SHORT CUTS

USING TEXTS TO EXPLORE ENGLISH

SHORT CUTS

USING TEXTS TO EXPLORE ENGLISH

By Mel Calman and Ben Duncan

PENGUIN BOOKS

PENGUIN BOOKS

Published by the Penguin Group
Penguin Books Ltd, 27 Wrights Lane, London W8 5TZ, England
Penguin Books USA Inc., 375 Hudson Street, New York, New York 10014, USA
Penguin Books Australia Ltd, Ringwood, Victoria, Australia
Penguin Books Canada Ltd, 10 Alcorn Avenue, Toronto, Ontario, Canada M4V 3B2
Penguin Books (NZ) Ltd, 182–190 Wairau Road, Auckland 10, New Zealand

Penguin Books Ltd, Registered Offices: Harmondsworth, Middlesex, England

Published by Penguin Books 1995
10 9 8 7 6 5 4 3 2 1

Illustrations by Mel Calman

Printed in Great Britain by Butler and Tanner Ltd, Frome and London
Set in Bembo and Futura

It's likely that father's interest in EFL was inspired partly by the fact that, with his dark hair and eyes, he was often mistaken for a foreigner himself. People in shops or cafés sometimes addressed him slowly, as if he didn't speak English. Bus conductors would ask helpfully, 'Do you know where you want to go?'

He was more amused than annoyed, and occasionally exaggerated the role of confused tourist, hamming it up shamelessly – and satirically – for his and our enjoyment. The combination of his east European parentage and British birth made him, while critical of English reserve, extremely proud to live in a country so relatively tolerant of racial differences.

He met Ben Duncan in 1962 and over a 30-year friendship they relentlessly engaged in their two favourite pastimes: the rather un-English pursuit of talking and the very English one of tea. Editing material for teachers was less a career move than a kind of pleasurable bonus. They were in the middle of *Short Cuts* when Mel died suddenly. It's good to know that, amidst the shock and the sadness, the work of this unique Anglo-European-American partnership will continue to be enjoyed by many. And who knows, as he used to say: you might even learn something . . .

Claire and Stephanie Calman

INTRODUCTION

A NOTE TO TEACHERS FROM BEN DUNCAN – ABOUT THIS BOOK

The idea for this book was Mel Calman's and this book is the result of a collaboration between us. Our hope was to produce something different from other books in several ways. As a cartoonist and journalist, Mel Calman contributed his own work and helped to choose a varied range of the best of other people's. In constructing the book, we were guided by the following thoughts.

- *Bits of English writing that are funny, or at any rate entertaining, are more likely to interest and motivate students* and we've chosen the texts in this book with that in mind. They are aimed at mid-intermediate level upwards. Some of the texts are obviously easier than others and they get progressively more difficult. They are examples of some of the best contemporary writing in English and the later texts are the sort students must expect to meet in examinations. Above all other considerations, we have tried to represent the English language as it actually is.

- *Drawings mixed up with, and related to, the texts are not only fun in themselves but they help to bridge gaps in students' knowledge.* Additionally, throughout this book, students are asked to draw. Like many teachers, I have begun to find that as a change from word-emphasizing activities drawing offers a great release. I have also found that Mel Calman's drawings, in particular, make students itch to try their own skills. I would rather encourage and make use of this, than have them doodling when I want them to concentrate on something else!

- *Students can only progress when they take responsibility for their own learning and feel themselves an important part of the teaching process.* A big step forward in language teaching in the last ten years has been the increasing awareness that students respond best when they are allowed to take control of their own learning. In my work as an assessor for the University of Cambridge teaching examinations, I have seen, more and more frequently, teachers asking their students to make suggestions about which direction the class should take and monitor their own progress. The students react with enthusiasm and creativity. Throughout this book we have included exercises where students are asked to create and stage activities of their own.

● *Integrating language skills – listening, speaking, reading and writing – is vital to successful teaching* and it is now commonplace in current teaching theory. The activities in this book are intended to encourage students in the use of these skills and they are designed to be communicative, with students working in pairs and groups.

Exploring the Texts

In my many years running seminars for teachers of English from abroad, I have found that we all agreed that the best method for exploiting texts is in some ways the most traditional.

1 Provide a context for the text – this arouses interest and assists comprehension by giving students some idea of what to expect.
2 Give students something to do whilst they read: something to look for, note down and be prepared to report upon. As well as providing signposts this, of course, provides the additional benefit of teaching students to read for a purpose.
3 Once students have grasped the general ideas of the passage, provide them with further work to explore the language of the text in more detail.

In this book, for each of these three stages, we have provided a selection of different activities and exercises from which teachers can pick and choose, adapting as necessary for different classroom situations and teaching styles. So, if an activity used for one text appeals strongly to you and your students – for example, matching or classifying – you can quickly and easily devise such activities for other texts.

The activities are designed to be diagnostic – to reveal weaknesses in which students need additional work. For example, the exercise on word order comes in Unit 1 because it shows up so many problems, covering so many different structures.

We've tried to make this book a pleasure to use and we've tried to judge every text and every activity on whether they are fun, challenging and relevant to students' experience, as well as being worthwhile in language terms.

Exploring English should be fun and the process of teaching works best when it is least painful. Help your students not to be too serious – when they're laughing, they're learning!

CONTENTS

UNIT I: YOURSELF AND OTHER
           PEOPLE

One: **Yourself and Us**   3
           autobiographical sketches by Mel and
           Ben

Two: **Other People**   9
           extract from *Goodbye to Berlin* by
           Christopher Isherwood

Three: **Your Health and Your Doctor**   14
           The Germ, a poem by Ogden Nash
           At the mercy of a child's plastic sword, an
           article by Miles Kington

Four: **The Words We Use About**   20
           Ourselves and Others
           extracts from *The Officially Politically
           Correct Dictionary and Handbook* by
           Henry Beard and Christopher Cerf
           Mural for restaurant gets artist in dogfight,
           an article by Charles Laurence

Five: **What Our Clothes Say About**   29
           Ourselves and Others
           Opera Buffa, a letter by George Bernard
           Shaw

Six: **How We See People of Other Age**   37
           Groups – Children
           Lost Eden, a strip cartoon by Posy
           Simmonds
           cartoon by Giles

Seven: **How We See People of Other Age** 44
Groups – Teenagers
extract from *Love and Friendship* by
Alison Lurie
extract from *The War Between the Tates*
by Alison Lurie

Eight: **What Language Can Tell About Us** 52
and Other People
It's a vunderful, vunderful book, an article by
Richard Guilliatt

UNIT II: YOUR COUNTRY AND
OTHER COUNTRIES

One: **Understanding Your Own Country** 61
The British Character, a cartoon by Pont
Moving addresses, an article by Keith
Waterhouse

Two: **Looking Beyond Your Own** 68
Country
Local body in identity crisis, an article by
Stephanie Calman

Three: **Exploring Your Own Country** 74
two extracts from *The Lost Continent* by
Bill Bryson

Four: **Exploring Other Countries** 80
extract from *Inca-Kola* by Matthew
Parris

Five: **Encountering People From Your** 87
Own Country Abroad
two scenes from *Some Americans Abroad*,
a play by Richard Nelson

Six: **Exploring Other Cultures**   95
                Arranged marriage, an article by Meera
                Syall

Seven: **Exploring National Attitudes**   103
                two extracts from *Hands off my baby!*,
                an article by Vicki Wood

Eight: **Comparing National Attitudes**   110
                three extracts from *Inglese* by Beppe
                Severgnini
                They are loud, late and don't tell the truth,
                an article by Sonia Purnell

Nine: **Changing Nationality**   119
                Expatriate Games, an article by Jonathan
                Wilson
                Waiting in room 3–120, an article by
                Kennedy Fraser

UNIT III: THE CHANGING WORLD

One: **Exploring the Changing World**   129
                cartoons by Roz Chast, Donald Reilly
                and Dedini

Two: **Changing Technology**   135
                cartoon by W. Miller
                Philip Norman on life without a flex, an
                article by Philip Norman

Three: **The Technology of Numbers**   142
                Reflections on a Royalty Statement, a poem
                by Wendy Cope

Four: **The Changing Language**   148
                Broken English, an article by Calvin
                Trillin

Five: **The Changing World of Pop Music**   158
Ringo Starr talks to Giles Smith about
shaking off the past, an article by Giles
Smith
If all you hear is radio gaga . . ., an article
by Louise Gray
In 1965 fifteen of the thirty best-selling US
singles were British . . ., an article by Jim
White

Six: **Changing Styles**   171
Hostile Haircuts, an article by John
Updike, with a cartoon by Maurice
Vellecoop

Seven: **The Changing Roles of Men and**   178
                 Women
Not quite New Man but less of a chore than
Sloth, an article by Ruth Picardie

Key to Activities   187

Acknowledgements   207

UNIT 1

ONE: YOURSELF AND US

ACTIVITIES – STAGE 1:

1 Draw a picture of yourself. Use a whole sheet of paper. You will have five minutes to do this. You will be given no further help or instructions. Start now.

2 Put your pencil down. Look at your picture. Are you all head, all body, or a balance of the two? Which features of yourself have you made large, and which small? What are you wearing, if anything?

3 Get together with another student, and look at your picture together. Teachers of young children and child psychologists find children's drawings of themselves revealing. What do your pictures reveal about the way you see yourselves?

ACTIVITIES – STAGE 2:

1 'Tell me about yourself,' people say when you first meet them. But where do you start? What do you include? Write down three things about yourself which you would tell someone who had just asked about you.

2 Now get together with a partner and exchange the bits of information you have written down.

3 Discuss with the same partner *why* each of you chose to tell what you did. Look at this list of the kinds of things people often use to describe themselves to others. Which things on the list did you not include? Why? Because you think them unimportant? Are they really unimportant?

  – your age
  – your nationality
  – your job or other occupation
  – your interests
  – your ambitions

- your family and personal situation: parents, husband or wife, children, boy- or girlfriend
- where you live: city, country, house, flat
- what you most like doing
- what you most dislike doing
- what you like about yourself
- what you wish was different about yourself
- what you *actually* spend most of your time doing

ACTIVITIES – STAGE 3:

1 People who write books like this one order students around as though they owned them. *Read this. Answer that. Write it down. Discuss it.*

But who *are* these people who make you reveal things about yourself, yet tell you nothing about themselves? We thought you'd like to know something about us, Mel and Ben. So we've each written a paragraph or two about ourselves for you to read. As you read, try to do these two things:

- find something Mel and Ben have in common
- list as many ways as you can in which the two men are different from one another.

We suggest you put the differences into a list, like this:

MEL   BEN

When you report to the class on the differences, try to show off some of the ways you know to show **contrast** in English.
For example:

Ben is _____ but Mel is _____.
Mel is _____, whereas Ben is _____.
Ben _____; Mel, however, _____.

If you like, add some other ways that you know to do this, and to vary the structure you use as often as you can.

Mel

I was born in London, but my parents were foreigners. My father came from Russia and my mother from Lithuania. They met in London and produced three children. I am the youngest.

I was educated in Cambridge and then returned to London to go to art school. Eventually I became a cartoonist – without meaning to do so.

I've been married (and divorced) twice. I have two grown-up daughters, both of them involved in writing and publishing.

Most of my cartoons are about men and women, though I also make jokes about politicians (who are neither men nor women, but strange creatures from another planet . . .). I met Ben many years ago and we became friends. We look very different: he is tall and I am shortish. He is calm and I am volatile. We both feel slightly outside England, I think. Ben, because he comes from America, and me because of my parents. That helps us to relish the oddities and pleasures of life in England.

And so, you have this book, written and drawn by two people who enjoy England, but are observers.

Are you a cartoonist?

Yes – and I'm overdrawn *

* A PUN.
What is the other meaning of 'overdrawn'?

Ben

I envy people who can say who they are in a few simple words.
For me, that's not easy. Nationality? Well . . . I have two
passports. English and American, or the other way around – for I
was born in Birmingham, Alabama, but have lived most of my life
5   in England, near Cambridge.

Occupation? I'm an ex-everything. Director of a large
advertising agency, theatre press officer, porter in a hospital,
broadcaster, cookery writer. One summer I even worked as a
cowboy. When things got really desperate, I sank to being a
10   teacher of English to foreign students.

Since that was the job I actually liked best, let's say I'm an ex-
teacher, now a freelance writer. I'm very sociable, but perhaps I'm
happiest alone, reading a book. I'm as tall as a basketball player,
but I hate all sports except swimming. Now, if I've confused you,
15   imagine what it's like being me!

Mel is SHORT, Ben is tall.

ACTIVITIES – STAGE 4:

1 When you've finished reading and discussing Mel's text and Ben's, you should be ready to consider some important questions about the way you read English, or any other language you are learning.

- Do you use a dictionary? A bilingual or an English/English dictionary?
- What are the advantages and disadvantages of each kind of dictionary?
- Do you look up every word? Do you guess at meaning?
- Do you write down and try to remember every new word you meet?
- When you record a word you want to learn, what else beside the meaning do you note down?

Your teacher will divide you into groups to discuss these questions, and then you will report back to the whole class.

2 List the words you don't know in the two texts. Using the answers to the questions above as a guide, divide them into the words you don't think you need to remember, and words you want to learn.

With the second list (those you want to learn), try with a partner to guess at the meaning, and then tell the class what you think the new words mean.

Throughout this book, we will be encouraging you to guess at the meanings of words. Here, for a start, are some examples of the ways in which the **context** of the word – the place in which it is used – can help you to work out the meaning.

(a) Ben worked as a *porter* in a hospital. Since this comes in a list of jobs, it is obviously something you do to earn money. Since Ben has no medical qualifications, he was obviously not a doctor or nurse. What kinds of work could a young man in these circumstances do in a hospital? So what is a porter?

(b) Mel says that Ben is calm, but he (Mel) is volatile. Because of the *but*, you know that *volatile* must be the opposite of *calm*. So what is the meaning of volatile?

(c) Mel says that the fact that both of them are from outside England means that they both *relish* the oddities and pleasures of life in England. Is *relish* here a noun/adjective/adverb/

verb? Is its meaning positive or negative? Can you think of one simple English word that is a near-synonym? What about e _ _ _ _? List some things that you *relish*.

3 Look at Ben's text. Like many texts in English, it begins with a general idea, and then supplies some details. The general idea is often contained in what is sometimes called a **topic sentence**, but in Ben's first paragraph the idea is in two sentences. What are they? Using the form below, and writing short notes, try to analyse the paragraph.

The supporting details

The general idea

4 Now, using this same plan for a paragraph, write about yourself. Begin with a topic sentence, or sentences, which express a general idea about the kind of person you are. Then supply some details which prove the generalization. Be sure that your last sentence sounds like an ending.

TWO: OTHER PEOPLE

ACTIVITIES – STAGE 1:

1 Christopher Isherwood, an Englishman then in his twenties, went to Berlin in 1929 and lived by teaching English. The book he wrote about this period of his life, *Goodbye to Berlin*, has been made into a musical, *Cabaret*, and a film. As a writer he is famous for noting the details of the way people speak and behave – as well as the way they look and dress – that reveal most about themselves.

Read this passage from *Goodbye to Berlin*. Record, in not more than about twenty-five words, your impressions of the three people we meet in the passage, Fritz, Sally and Christopher. You do not have to write whole sentences, just odd words. Try to use your own words, not Christopher Isherwood's.

One afternoon, early in October, I was invited to black coffee at Fritz Wendel's flat. Fritz always invited you to 'Black coffee,' with emphasis on the black. He was very proud of his coffee. People used to say that it was the strongest in Berlin.

Fritz himself was dressed in his usual coffee-party costume – a very thick white yachting sweater and very light blue flannel trousers. He greeted me with his full-lipped, luscious smile:

"'lo, Chris!'

'Hullo, Fritz. How are you?'

'Fine.' He bent over the coffee-machine, his sleek black hair unplastering itself from his scalp and falling in richly scented locks over his eyes. 'This darn thing doesn't go,' he added.

'How's business?' I asked.

'Lousy and terrible.' Fritz grinned richly. 'Or I pull off a new deal in the next month or I go as a gigolo.'

'*Either* . . . or . . .,' I corrected, from force of professional habit.

'I'm speaking a lousy English just now,' drawled Fritz, with great self-satisfaction. 'Sally says maybe she'll give me a few lessons.'

'Who's Sally?'

'Why, I forgot. You don't know Sally. Too bad of me. Eventually she's coming around here this afternoon.'

'Is she nice?'

Fritz rolled his naughty black eyes, handing me a rum-moistened
cigarette from his patent tin:

'*Mar*-vellous!' he drawled. 'Eventually I believe I'm getting crazy
about her.'

'And who is she? What does she do?'

'She's an English girl, an actress: sings at the Lady Windermere
– hot stuff, believe me!'

'That doesn't sound much like an English girl, I must say.'

'Eventually she's got a bit of French in her. Her mother was
French.'

A few minutes later, Sally herself arrived.

'Am I terribly late, Fritz darling?'

'Only half of an hour, I suppose,' Fritz drawled, beaming with
proprietary pleasure. 'May I introduce Mr Isherwood – Miss
Bowles? Mr Isherwood is commonly known as Chris.'

'I'm not,' I said. 'Fritz is about the only person who's ever called
me Chris in my life.'

Sally laughed. She was dressed in black silk, with a small cape
over her shoulders and a little cap like a page-boy's stuck jauntily
on one side of her head:

'Do you mind if I use your telephone, sweet?'

'Sure. Go right ahead.' Fritz caught my eye. 'Come into the
other room, Chris. I want to show you something.' He was
evidently longing to hear my first impressions of Sally, his new
acquisition.

'For heaven's sake, don't leave me alone with this man!' she
exclaimed. 'Or he'll seduce me down the telephone. He's most
terribly passionate.'

As she dialled the number, I noticed that her finger-nails were
painted emerald green, a colour unfortunately chosen, for it called
attention to her hands, which were much stained by cigarette-
smoking and as dirty as a little girl's. She was dark enough to be
Fritz's sister. Her face was long and thin, powdered dead white.
She had very large brown eyes which should have been darker, to
match her hair and the pencil she used for her eyebrows.

'Hilloo,' she cooed, pursing her brilliant cherry lips as though
she were going to kiss the mouthpiece: 'Ist das Du, mein Liebling?'
Her mouth opened in a fatuously sweet smile.

Christopher Isherwood,
Goodbye to Berlin

ACTIVITIES – STAGE **2**:

1 Now read the passage again, and, as you do, note some of the physical details given about Fritz and Sally, and then try to say what these tell you about their characters. One example of a detail is given for each person to help you to get started.

Detail	What it tells you about Fritz	Detail	What it tells you about Sally
Dressed in thick white yachting sweater		Dressed in black silk	

2 Because Christopher Isherwood taught English, he notices the mistakes Fritz makes. In line 16 he corrects *or . . . or* to *either . . . or*. Can you find a few more of Fritz's mistakes and correct them?

The mistake	The correct or better way to say it

3 In line 17, *drawled* is obviously a way of speaking. From the rest of what you know about Fritz, do you think it means:

(a) in a high, unpleasant voice
(b) in a slow, sexy voice
(c) so quietly you can hardly hear him?

   Find two other words for ways of speaking, and try to work out what they mean from the way they are used in the passage.

ACTIVITIES – STAGE 3:

1 When you discuss or write about a passage like this one, you will, inevitably, use adjectives. (You've probably already done this in some of the exercises you've completed.) In English, adjectives have a strict order in which they appear before the noun.

> Fritz was wearing a   *thick*   *white*   *yachting*   *sweater*

Adjectives which are to do with **fact** go nearest to the noun. Those which are of **opinion** go further away.

A yachting sweater is a *kind* of sweater: no argument. White is pretty factual, too. Thick is more a matter of opinion. We know from the passage that Sally is English, that she is pretty, that she is young. Put these three adjectives into the correct order to describe her, in a sentence.

Now, write a three-adjective description of Fritz, and then of Christopher. Look back at your notes for questions 1 and 2, Activities, stage 2. You may use your own adjectives, or choose some from this list:

intelligent	*conceited*	*young*	*observant*	*overdressed*
dark	*talkative*	*poor*	*hospitable*	*well-educated*

Fritz is a/an _____ _____ _____ German.

Christopher   is   a/an   _____   _____   _____ Englishman.

2 Order of adjectives is, of course, not the only problem of word order in English. Individual words like adverbs, and parts of sentences like subject and verb also have a strict order which is often different from your own language.

Look at this sentence:

> *Fritz always invited you to black coffee.*

Put the grammar names below by the parts of the sentence they describe.

Adverb of frequency

Verb

Subject

Preposition phrase expanding the meaning of the verb

Object

Then work out why these parts come in the order they do in this sentence.

Especially when you are about to do some writing, it helps to remind yourself of what you know already about word order. These ideas may help you.

(a) In a class of mixed nationalities, get together with others who speak your language, or work on your own. Tell the class one important way in which English word order is different from yours.

(b) In a class of a single nationality, work in pairs to decide which difference in word order is the most difficult to remember, and give an example in your language, and in English.

(c) Finally, make a short list of the differences you try to remember when you write in English.

3 The passage records the very strong impression that Sally made upon Christopher Isherwood at their first meeting. Imagine yourself making such a strong impression upon a young writer, meeting you for the first time. Write a short passage in which he (or she) describes you. Look back at your notes on the way Sally dresses, talks, the things she does. Include all these details about yourself. Include some adjectives. Include some dialogue (some things that you say). Note carefully how the dialogue in the passage is **punctuated**.

THREE: YOUR HEALTH AND YOUR DOCTOR

ACTIVITIES – STAGE 1:

1 English speakers generally begin a conversation with people they haven't seen lately by asking, 'How are you?' but the last thing they expect is for anyone to answer the question by giving an account of their health. Do you ask such a question in your language? Do you actually answer it? Is your health, or health and medicine in general regarded as a possible subject of polite conversation?

2 Read this poem by the American writer Ogden Nash. At the end, are you clear about what a *germ* is, and what the word for it is in your language?

Infirm is a slightly unusual word for *ill* – some hospitals are called *infirmaries*.

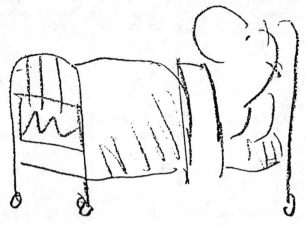

Pachyderm is an uncommon, technical word, but English speakers know it means *elephant*. Please draw an elephant, and show it to the student next to you, to be sure you agree which animal it is!

The Germ

A mighty creature is the germ,
Though smaller than the pachyderm
His customary dwelling place
Is deep within the human race.
His childish pride he often pleases
By giving people strange diseases.
Do you, dear reader, feel infirm?
You probably contain a germ.

Ogden Nash,
Bed Riddance

5

ACTIVITIES – STAGE 2:

1 Look at the rhythm of the lines in the poem, which looks something like this:

2 Try, with your partner, to write a couplet – just two lines – in this rhythm, on the subject of health. Try to make it rhyme (*place/race, pleases/diseases* are examples). You may take rhyming words from the poem, if you like, or make up some of your own.

ACTIVITIES – STAGE **3**:

1 Now you are going to read a text by Miles Kington, who writes a regular column in the London daily newspaper *The Independent*. As you read, try to answer the question below. (Don't try so hard that you fail to enjoy the text – just watch for the answers to appear.)

● Miles Kington says he told the doctor some lies. What were they?

At the mercy of a child's plastic sword

The other day I attempted to deceive a doctor. Yes, I told a doctor several lies. A doctor I hardly knew, at that. It happened like this. I have recently changed doctors. Nothing wrong with the old doctor, but I wanted to show that freedom of choice means
5   something. So I changed doctors. And the new doctor said that all new patients got free medical check-ups. Not if they wanted them, but if they wanted them or not.

   This slightly shook me, I have to say. Once doctors start checking up on you, they are liable to find something wrong with
10   you, and then they try to put it right, and I really don't have the time to get involved in a full-blown doctor–patient ongoing healing relationship situation.

   Luckily, it wasn't a health check-up at all. It was a health lecture. You know, the doctor takes your blood pressure and pretends to
15   listen to your pulse, and then starts asking personal questions about your habits such as, do you smoke? Uh huh. Do you drink? Uh huh. How many different drugs do you habitually ingest? I see . . .

   I gave up smoking some time ago and the only drugs I take are
20   those forced on me by doctors, so it's just the drinking question I take time to answer. Usually I say, Oh, just a couple of glasses after sundown. Then they stare sternly and say: And how many *before* sundown, Mr Kington? Then I storm out saying I have never been so insulted in all my life, and change doctors again.

Actually, the drinking question is quite easy to answer. You   25
estimate your drinking at roughly half what it really is. They then
double it to compensate for your lying and hey presto. It's the
people who tell the truth who are in trouble. Nobody believes
them.

That wasn't the question I lied in answer to, anyway. I'm just   30
giving you a bit of background atmosphere. No, it was the next
question that led me into the paths of untruth: 'What exercise do
you take?'

'I cycle every day,' I said, 'and go swimming now and then. I
don't play games, though. That's it.'   35

'Excellent,' said the doctor. 'Cycling is one of the best forms of
exercise there is. Good!'

She was obviously also pretty pleased that I had given up
competitive games, because after all things like rugby and cricket
cause more ill health than any good they do.   40

It wasn't till I was back home that I realised I had told less than
the truth. The moment of dawning came when my son (aged four)
approached me brandishing a large plastic sword crying: 'En
garde, Dad!' This is part of a ritual we have worked out between
us. He shouts his warning (the only French he knows). I then have   45
five seconds in which to a) locate another plastic sword, b) get it
into my hand, c) raise it to ward off the savage swish at my midriff.
If I don't do all three, I d) get thwacked with a plastic sword and
die, rolling over again and again, groaning horribly, until I a)
squash the cat or b) fall down the cellar steps.   50

However much I exclaim in pain, he knows it does not hurt,
because he has watched cartoons of violence and knows that Tom
does not hurt Jerry. Ergo, he does not hurt me. So when we have
our sword fights or cushion fights or re-enact SuperTed, Batman
and Dangermouse fights, I have to exert all my strength and   55
ingenuity not to hurt a) myself and, I suppose, though he's in much
less danger than I am, b) him.

To put it another way, when the doctor asked me what exercise I
took, I should have said: 'Well, there's cushion fighting, mortal
combat of all kinds, chasing to the death, being jumped on out of   60
a tree by Robin Hood, being crushed to death by dinosaurs, dying
slowly in picturesque and horrible fashions . . .'

Miles Kington,
The Independent
31 March 1992

ACTIVITIES – STAGE **4**:

1 Here are some exercises to help you with vocabulary in the text.

(a) Find the place in the text where Miles Kington uses nine words that make fun of some of the over-fancy language people in the English-speaking countries (especially Americans, and more especially Californians) use when talking about themselves, their work, their love affairs.

(b) Find an uncommon word which sounds like technical medical language, but which means simply *take* or *use*.

(c) Find a verb that imitates the sound of something hitting something else with a loud noise.

(d) Find a noun that imitates the sound of something moving through the air very fast.

(e) Find a verb (here an *-ing* form) that imitates the sound someone makes when suffering.

2 Here are some further exercises to help you to extend your own vocabulary.

First, draw a picture of a man.

It can be very simple, like this one Mel has drawn, but make him bigger, using a whole sheet of paper, and give him longer arms and legs, please!

Early in your studies of English, you learn words for parts of the body, like *arm, leg* and so on.

But there is a much larger vocabulary of other often-used words like *midriff* (line 47). Try to put the word *midriff* in the right place on your drawing. Then try to add some other such words that you know, and test your partner to see if he or she can point to the right place. Your teacher will guide you about which of these words you could say anywhere, and which you could only use with people you know well.

Examples of some less common words for parts of the body:

shin (not *chin*)   *thigh*   *palm*   *nape*

3 Again, early in your studies you are taught to say, 'I have a headache/pain in my back,' and so on. But very often we are much more vague about what is wrong with us. Here are some expressions we use when we talk to the doctor in that situation. Can you add to them?

out of sorts   not myself   under the weather
not one hundred per cent   a few degrees under

With your partner, prepare a short (between eight and ten lines) dialogue to perform for the class. One of you is the patient and the other is the doctor. The patient describes his troubles, the doctor asks questions. Use some of the words and expressions you have learned.

The patient should tell one lie.

When the class hears your dialogue, they will try to guess which line of the patient's dialogue is the lie.

4 Think of an activity, involving either speaking or writing or both, in which you practise some of the material in this section.

One possibility: extend your dialogue to twenty-five or thirty lines and write it as homework. Another: write a text like Miles Kington's, in which you tell the doctor something not strictly true, and then tell your reader what really happened. But try to think of your own way of revising the lesson, bearing in mind the people in the class, their ages, jobs, interests, and so on.

FOUR: THE WORDS WE USE ABOUT OURSELVES AND OTHERS

ACTIVITIES – STAGE 1:

1 Few descriptive words in any language are completely fair or neutral. Most have either pleasant or unpleasant meanings. Look back at the description of yourself you did in Chapter One, either in the notes on your drawing, or in the paragraph you wrote. Can you see examples of words you chose which could be made more negative or more positive? For example, a *slim* person sounds attractive, a *thin* one less so.

2 Some groups of people in every country of the world have words used about them which show that the speaker – the person using the words – thinks poorly about them. Here are some examples of the general kinds of groups of people of whom unpleasant words are used. Can you think of any such words, which may be slang or may be correct everyday English? Write the words down by the name of the group.

- Skin colour or race
- Job
- Sex (male, female)
- Religion
- Education
- Sexual orientation (heterosexual, homosexual, bisexual)
- Physical type or shape
- Intelligence
- Physical condition or ability
- Age (*any* age)
- Financial position
- Marital status
- Marital status of parents

3 Alone, think of one fact about yourself which could be the subject of an unpleasant description. (Few of us are so perfect that *nothing* is wrong!) Write down one way in English of stating this fact which is negative, another more positive. Your teacher will go

around the class to help you as you work. When you are ready, *only* those who wish to will put their words on the board. Those who prefer not to, do not have to.

4 In all English-speaking countries, there is now a powerful movement to change the way we think, speak and write about some of these groups. This attempt is often called the movement to political correctness (sometimes shortened to PC). The movement itself arouses feelings as powerful as some of the language it tries to change. Is anything similar to this happening in your country?

5 Read now some definitions selected by us from *The Officially Politically Correct Dictionary and Handbook*, by Henry Beard and Christopher Cerf, published in 1992. Many of them sound almost incredible, but the authors found them all in published writings.

Here are a few things to do as you read.

(a) Look back at some of the groups we considered in Activity 3, earlier. How many of the groups listed are covered by the definitions? Put them in one list. Put in another the groups you were surprised to find in the definitions.

(b) You will (we hope) realize that many English speakers think that some of these definitions are exaggerated and absurd, while others have become standard, everyday English.

Put a check (✓) by those which you expect to find in the English you now read and hear. Those you think are funny, indicate by drawing a smile (◡) beside them.

African-American The Smith College Office of Student Affairs defines 'African-American' as 'one of several concepts that refer to those citizens of the United States who are of African descent.' It is generally considered more appropriate than 'black' because it
5 implies a connection with the home continent and because, as linguistics expert Robert B. Moore puts it, 'the symbolism of white as positive and black as negative [is] pervasive in our culture.' Nonetheless, the term 'African-American' should be used with caution, warn the Fellows of the University of Missouri Journalism
10 School's Multicultural Management Program, since 'it may be objectionable to those persons preferring black.'

Alternative dentation False teeth.

Alternatively schooled Uneducated; illiterate.

Animal companion Pet. Ingrid Newkirk,
15 national director of People for the Ethical Treatment of Animals, prefers 'companion animal.' According to *U.S. News & World Report*, both
20 these terms are coming into disrepute because they are **anthropocentric**; i.e., they imply that the human role in the relationship is
25 somehow superior. Proponents of this point of view suggest such alternatives
30 as 'friend' or **protector**. The word **companion**,

standing alone, is also recommended in some circles, but, since
the term may also be used as a nonheterosexist, gender-free   35
substitute for 'lover,' caution is advised.

Asian-American The Smith College Office of Student Affairs
defines this as 'a self-definition reflecting the common identity,
similar treatment, and shared goals of those U.S. citizens of Asian
descent.' The word 'Oriental' is not acceptable, the Smith Office   40
continues, because it was bestowed 'by other people'—in this
case, by Europeans. 'Naming someone is a symbol of the power
one has over them to define who they are,' the Smith Office
concludes. 'Naming oneself reclaims that power.'

Aurally inconvenienced Hard-of-hearing; deaf. Also: **aurally**   45
challenged.

Chair Increasingly the preferred gender-inclusive substitute for
'chairman' or 'chairwoman,' according to usage experts Casey
Miller and Kate Swift. Example: *Charlene asked the* **chair** *to table*
the motion.   50

Chemically inconvenienced Under the influence of alcohol or
drugs. See also: sobriety-deprived.

Chicana/Chicano The preferred term for women and men,
respectively, of Mexican-American descent, created, according to
the Smith College Office of Student Affairs, 'to reflect their concern   55
about preserving their culture and heritage as opposed to
assimilating into the dominant Eurocentric culture of the U.S.A.'

Chronologically gifted Old. See also: **experientially enhanced;**
longer-living; mature; senior; seasoned.

Cosmetically different Ugly. Example: Todd's favorite politically   60
correct movie was *The Good, the Bad, and the* **Cosmetically**
Different.

Differently abled Physically or mentally disabled. In the words of
the Smith College Office of Student Affairs, the term was 'created
to underline the concept that differently abled individuals are just   65
that, not less or inferior in any way [as the terms disabled,
handicapped, etc. imply].' Also: **differently able**.

Differently advantaged Poor. Also: **economically exploited;**
economically marginalized.

Differently interesting Boring. Also: **charm-free**.   70

Genetically oppressive White.

Hair disadvantaged *The Japan Economic Journal's* term for 'bald,' rapidly gaining currency in the U.S. See also: **differently hirsute; follicularly challenged.**

75 **Herstory** The *Random House Webster's College Dictionary* defines this as 'History (used as an alternative form to distinguish or emphasize the particular experience of women).' *A Woman's New World Dictionary* amplifies this as '1. The past as seen through the eyes of women. 2. The removal of male self-

80 glorification from history.' However, Mary Daly, who teaches feminist ethics in the Department of Theology of Boston College, finds the term 'herstory' unacceptable, since it implies that the achievements of women constitute a separate, minor branch of the story of personkind.

85 **Incomplete success** Failure. The term was originally coined in 1980 by President Jimmy Carter to characterize the raid to free the American hostages in Iran.

Indefinitely idled Unemployed. See also: **in an orderly transition between career changes.**

90 **Larger-than-average citizen** One who might once have been characterized as fat. Also: **person of size; person of sub-stance.**

Least best Worst. A term used by the United Parcel Service in evaluating its drivers.

95 **Mentally challenged** A more sensitive substitute for the demeaning phrase 'mentally retarded.' Also an appropriate synonym for 'stupid.' See also: **cerebrally challenged.**

Morally different Dishonest; immoral; evil. See also: **ethically disoriented.**

100 **Motivationally deficient** Lazy. Because the word 'deficient' has the quality of 'blaming the victim' for a condition more properly attributed to the failures of society, this phrase is more and more frequently being replaced by the less judgmental **motivationally dispossessed.**

105 **Person of color, person of Color** A nonwhite person. This is an example of the 'people first' wordings currently receiving praise in liberation politics circles.

Person of gender A woman.

Person of noncolor A white person, especially a white Anglo-Saxon Protestant.

Sex worker The preferred occupational title for 'prostitute.' The term 'prostitute' is inappropriate, not only because it is judgmental, but because, as Dr. Dale Spender points out in *Women of Ideas and What Men Have Done to Them*, it is extremely difficult to define it without including 'wives,' who 'also exchange sexual services in return for support.' See also: **sex care provider; persons presenting themselves as commodity allotments within a business doctrine**.

Significant other Husband; lover; spouse; wife; girlfriend; boyfriend; sex partner.

Uniquely coordinated Clumsy.

Waitron The *Random House Webster's College Dictionary* defines this trendsetting new term as 'a person of either sex who waits on tables; waiter or waitress.' Example: 'Waitron, *there's a nonhuman animal in my soup!*' Also: **waitperson; dining-room attendant**.

Womyn An alternate spelling of 'women,' used, the *Random House Webster's College Dictionary* tells us, 'to avoid the suggestion of sexism in the sequence "m-e-n."'

> *Henry Beard and Christopher Cerf,*
> *The Officially Politically Correct*
> *Dictionary and Handbook*

ACTIVITIES – STAGE 2:

1 You can easily see how some of the new PC language is formed.

One common method is to combine an adverb (usually ending in -*ly*), or a noun, with an adjective (usually ending in -*ed*). From the definitions, find three examples of this construction.

Now, working with a partner, construct a politically correct term for someone usually described in a negative way. Use the construction above. Then write down the unpleasant, negative term often used about this person.

2 Your teacher will ask each pair to come to the board and write up the two terms. Try to imagine yourself the person described by these terms. (Close your eyes, and actually try to hear someone saying them to you.) Which would you prefer? The teacher will invite you to report your opinion to the class.

As you do this, remember that some groups of people actually *dislike* the new PC language, and deliberately call themselves by the older, more unpleasant terms.

3 One of the most argued-about parts of PC language concerns the names of jobs. Many of these which were traditionally done by men ended in *-man*. Now that they are often done by women, new words are found for the job, or old words changed. Similarly, many 'male' words like *air steward* at one time added *-ess* to describe women doing the same job, but have now been replaced by terms like *flight attendant*.

First, list some jobs ending in *-man*. Do you know how these are changed as more of these jobs are done by women? Example: *postman*.

Second, divide the class into men and women, two groups. Then, vote within the groups on the following statements: either Agree or Disagree.

(a) Women can do any job, even those usually done by men.

AGREE/DISAGREE

(b) Men can do any job, even those often done by women (hospital nurse, secretary, children's nurse).

AGREE/DISAGREE

(c) Names of jobs that do not define the sex of the person are an improvement on the old words.

AGREE/DISAGREE

4 Look at the words you checked (✓) as being genuine words you needed to know. Are they in your English/English dictionary? Are they in your bilingual dictionary? What can you do to keep your knowledge of English up to date?

ACTIVITIES – STAGE **3**:

1 Political correctness covers not just words, but pictures, too. Can you think of some ways that certain groups of people are shown in pictures which might be offensive?

2 Now we are going to read a short news story from the *Daily Telegraph*. So that you can read quickly and enjoy it, here are three key words to do with painting that you will find in the story. Match the words on the left with the definitions on the right:

mural	a painting which looks so real you forget it is a painting
portrait	a painting on a wall
trompe l'oeil	a painting of a real person or animal

Mural for restaurant gets artist in dogfight

A New York mural meant to simply brighten-up a local eyesore has become a monument to the extremes of racial sensitivity and political correctness, *writes Charles Laurence in New York.*

An artist, Audrey Sackstein, agreed to paint the boarded-up doorway of the once celebrated Lundy's Restaurant on the   5
waterfront of Sheepshead Bay, Brooklyn, with a *trompe l'oeil* view of the interior as in its 1950s heyday.

She planned to show waiters and customers with a mixture of black and white faces. But a Brooklyn historian, overseeing the Sheepshead Bay Beautification Programme, advised her to paint   10
the customers white and the waiters black to be historically accurate.

But within two days several black men complained. 'Some people still have the warped mentality that all black people can do is serve,' said one.   15

Mrs Sackstein promptly changed the mural to model No 2; black and white waiters, and black and white customers. But a vandal smeared black tar over the remaining white faces. The project director, local businessman and aspiring politician, Mr Peter Romeo, asked her to remove the entire mural.   20

Instead, she took out her paints again. Hoping to please everybody, she repainted all the faces as different breeds of dog. Her own black labrador-cross, Worf, is seen as a waiter in the rear left in model No. 3. 'I paint dog portraits professionally, and I thought that as everyone loves dogs, I would please everybody,'   25
she said.

But Mr Romeo feared those originally offended would now think they were being portrayed as dogs, and told her again to remove her work.

Two months after the paint dried, Mrs Sackstein's mural is   30 popular with passers-by. But it is there only because Mrs Sackstein, whose husband is a lawyer, threatened Mr Romeo with a law suit if he removed her work without permission.

Charles Laurence,
The Daily Telegraph
18 October 1993

ACTIVITIES – STAGE **4**:

1 The painting went through four versions. Please fill in the chart below to show you understand what happened to the people in the picture in each version.

	The waiters	**The customers**
When she first painted it		
After the protest		
What the vandals did		
Now		

2 As a final check, decide which of the following statements are true, which false.

- Audrey Sackstein painted her picture on the closed door of a restaurant which had been famous in the 1950s
- She tried to show the restaurant as it had been at that time
- The white customers objected to being shown as dogs
- Mr Peter Romeo was the owner of the restaurant
- The picture is now disliked by most people
- The picture only survives because Mrs Sackstein's husband is a lawyer, who would go to court if someone tried to get the picture removed.

FIVE: WHAT OUR CLOTHES SAY ABOUT OURSELVES AND OTHERS

ACTIVITIES – STAGE 1:

1 A writer whose work we will read later in this Unit, Alison Lurie, wrote a book called *The Language of Clothes*. In it, she suggests that we send out messages by what we wear. We also get messages from what other people wear, though not always what they intend. In this section, we are going to explore the kinds of judgments we make about people, based upon clothes.

To begin with, look at what *you* are wearing in the class today. Choose either one item of clothing, or a combination. Look at some of the messages below. *Either* select one which you think you are sending, based upon the item or items you have chosen; or write a similar one of your own. Stand up, indicate which item or items of clothing, and then report your message to the class.

Messages:

- I don't care at all what I wear
- My mother/husband/boyfriend/girlfriend chooses what I wear, and I take no interest in it
- I've just bought this/these new _____, I paid a lot for it/them, and I'm very proud of it/them
- This _____ goes with my eyes/hair/new suntan and that's why I'm wearing it
- This was the last clean _____ I own so I had to wear it
- I got up so late and dressed so fast I didn't notice what I put on and I wish you hadn't mentioned it

2 Can you think of (a) groups of people who all dress alike, in uniforms, and (b) situations in which everyone is expected to wear the same clothes?

Now look at your list of people who wear uniforms. Do the uniforms send a message? What message? Look at your list of situations where people are expected to wear the same clothes. Are they sending a message to each other? What message?

3 Now we are going to read a famous letter about clothes. In many English-speaking countries, people write to the editor of a newspaper on some subject which the writer feels strongly about. The newspaper best-known for its letter section is the London *Times* (as it happens, the newspaper of which Mel is the cartoonist!).

Is there such a custom in your country? Have you ever written to the editor of a newspaper? Was your letter published?

4 The letter you are going to read was written to *The Times* by George Bernard Shaw. He lived from 1856–1950, and was one of the most famous British playwrights. In his early working life, he was a drama and music critic, and this letter tells about something that happened to him at the opera. This time, as you read, *do not* write anything. Instead, get out a blank piece of paper and a pencil.

George Bernard Shaw had a problem at the opera. Draw a picture of what the problem was.

Opera Buffa

From Mr Bernard Shaw

Sir,

The Opera management at Covent Garden regulates the dress of its male patrons. When is it going to do the same to the women?

On Saturday night I went to the Opera. I wore the costume imposed on me by the regulations of the house. I fully recognize the advantage of those regulations. Evening dress is cheap, simple, durable, prevents rivalry and extravagance on the part of male leaders of fashion, annihilates class distinctions, and gives men who are poor and doubtful of their social position (that is, the great majority of men) a sense of security and satisfaction that no clothes of their own choosing could confer, besides saving a whole sex the trouble of considering what they should wear on state occasions. The objections to it are as dust in the balance in the eyes of the ordinary Briton. These objections are that it is colourless and characterless; that it involves a whitening process which makes the shirt troublesome, slightly uncomfortable, and seriously unclean; that it acts as a passport for undesirable persons; that it fails to guarantee sobriety, cleanliness, and order on the part of the wearer; and that it reduces to a formula a very vital human

habit which should be the subject of constant experiment and   20
active private enterprise.

All such objections are thoroughly un-English . . .

Every argument that applies to the regulation of the man's dress
applies equally to the regulation of the woman's. Now let me
describe what actually happened to me at the Opera. Not only   25
was I in evening dress by compulsion, but I voluntarily added
many graces of conduct as to which the management made no
stipulation whatever. I was in my seat in time for the first chord of
the overture. I did not chatter during the music nor raise my voice
when the Opera was too loud for normal conversation. I did not   30
get up and go out when the statue music began. My language was
fairly moderate considering the number and nature of the
improvements on Mozart volunteered by Signor Caruso, and the
respectful ignorance of the dramatic points of the score exhibited
by the conductor and the stage manager – if there is such a   35
functionary at Covent Garden. In short, my behaviour was
exemplary.

At 9 o'clock (the Opera began at 8) a lady came in and sat
down very conspicuously in my line of sight. She remained there
until the beginning of the last act. I do not complain of her coming   40
late and going early; on the contrary, I wish she had come later
and gone earlier. For this lady, who had very black hair, had stuck
over her right ear the pitiable corpse of a large white bird, which
looked exactly as if someone had killed it by stamping on its
breast, and then nailed it to the lady's temple, which was   45
presumably of sufficient solidity to bear the operation. I am not, I
hope, a morbidly squeamish person; but the spectacle sickened
me. I presume that if I had presented myself at the doors with a
dead snake round my neck, a collection of blackbeetles pinned to
my shirtfront, and a grouse in my hair, I should have been refused   50
admission. Why, then, is a woman to be allowed to commit such a
public outrage? Had the lady been refused admission, as she
should have been, she would have soundly rated the tradesman
who imposed the disgusting head-dress on her under the false
pretence that 'the best people' wear such things, and withdrawn   55
her custom from him; and thus the root of the evil would be struck
at: for your fashionable woman generally allows herself to be
dressed according to the taste of a person whom she would not let
sit down in her presence. I once, in Drury Lane Theatre, sat behind
a matinée hat decorated with the two wings of a seagull,   60
artificially reddened at the joints so as to produce an illusion of

being freshly plucked from a live bird. But even that lady stopped
short of the whole seagull. Both ladies were evidently regarded by
their neighbours as ridiculous and vulgar; but that is hardly enough
when the offence is one which produces a sensation of physical
65   sickness in persons of normal humane sensibility.

I suggest to the Covent Garden authorities that, if they feel
bound to protect their subscribers against the danger of my
shocking them with a blue tie, they are at least equally bound to
protect me against the danger of a woman shocking me with a
70   dead bird.

Yours truly,
G. BERNARD SHAW

ACTIVITIES – STAGE 2:

1 In groups, compare your pictures. Do you agree about the
problem? Choose which is the best picture in your group. Then
your teacher will put up those you have
chosen, and you will vote to decide
which is the best picture in the class.
Here is a drawing Mel did of
a similar situation. It is
different in at least one
important way from
the situation Shaw
describes. What is
the difference?

ACTIVITIES – STAGE 3:

1 Here are two extremes of the styles of language in which people write English. It should be easy for you to circle the group that describes the kind of language Shaw uses in this letter.

1	2
Casual	Over-elaborate
Relaxed	Very formal
Conversational	Complicated
Simple	Literary
Colloquial	Heavy
Light	Indirect

This difference in style, which is sometimes called **register**, is important for you, as a student, to recognize. The second kind of language is often used, as Shaw uses it, to be deliberately comic. If you use it your reader may think you mean to be funny when in fact you mean the opposite!

2 Look at the examples below. Here are some translations into everyday (but perfectly correct) English of some of the things Shaw says in the letter. Find the words in Shaw's letter that correspond to the bits below.

Tells men what clothes they must wear

Robs you of the fun of choosing what to wear

Behaved well in ways not mentioned in the rules

Complained to the salesperson who sold her the hat

Makes normal people feel ill

ACTIVITIES – STAGE 4:

1 Even for students at your level, being polite in spoken English is sometimes difficult, because we use ways of saying things indirectly almost as complicated as some of Shaw's language in the letter.

Imagine you are sitting behind the woman in the hat at the opera. What exact words would you use to ask her to remove it?

2 Here are some other situations which might happen at the opera. Working with a partner, decide both what you would say, and what the other person might say in reply. If you can, add one more situation that might occur at the opera, or at a theatre or cinema.

- When you find the seats with your numbers on them, someone is already sitting in them.
- The person sitting next to you sings the opera along with the singers on the stage.
- You have ordered your drinks for the interval in advance. Just as you arrive to collect them, you see someone else picking them up.
- The person sitting next to you tells the whole story of the opera to his companion.
- As you are leaving, the person next to you picks up your coat instead of his own.

ACTIVITIES – STAGE 5:

1 Write a letter to the editor of *The Times*, in the exaggerated style of Shaw's letter. The letter should be about one of the following subjects.

(a) Learning English, and the English language.
(b) Something that happened on a recent visit to an English-speaking country.
(c) Getting to know an English-speaking person or family.
(d) Working for an English or American company in an English-speaking situation.
(e) Something odd or strange that happened to you at the opera or theatre or cinema in an English-speaking country.

2 If you actually want to *send* your letter (and why not?) your teacher will give you the address you need.

ACTIVITIES – STAGE 6:

1 At your level, although you know the vocabulary of clothes, you may want to do some revision, especially as the words used for clothes in English are changing so fast (and so are the clothes themselves!) Look at the items below, and then put them into the correct column, either FORMAL or CASUAL. (Some items may go in both columns.) Try to add as many other words as you can, from your own vocabulary. By each item, write M for clothes only men usually wear, F for clothes only women usually wear, MF for clothes both wear.

trainers	jewellery	blazer	bow tie
tie	cardigan	sweatpants	denim skirt
dinner jacket	button-down shirt	polo shirt	
blouse	sweatshirt	linen jacket	
chinos	T-shirt	cords	
suit	leather jacket	jeans	

FORMAL	CASUAL

2 Some places now have *dress codes*; restaurants, discos, bars, for instance. These are rules about what you must wear, like the rule Shaw mentions in his letter. Do you ever go to such places? Name some of them, and describe their dress codes. Are there places – offices, for instance – where there is a dress code which is unofficial and never stated, but still important? Do you and your friends have a dress code which you never mention but all observe?

3 Finally, look back briefly at some of the language Shaw uses about the woman in the hat, and about women in general. Then discuss the following questions.

- Would he use the same language about men?
- What message about women is he sending?
- What message about himself?
- The musical play (and film) *My Fair Lady* is based on one of Shaw's plays. The main character, a (male) professor, sings a comic song called 'Why can't a Woman be More Like a Man?'. Can you see any connection between that song, and Shaw's letter?

SIX: HOW WE SEE PEOPLE OF OTHER AGE GROUPS – CHILDREN

ACTIVITIES – STAGE 1:

1 Discuss these questions in pairs or groups (your teacher will organize these) and then report to the class.

- Is your experience of children based upon:
  - younger brothers or sisters
  - your own children
  - children within your large family, like nieces and nephews
  - your work as a teacher or similar job?
- What kind of language do you use when:
  - talking about children
  - talking to children? (You may want to look back at your notes on Chapter Four.)
- Do you regard children as being:
  - in danger from the world around them
  - a danger themselves to your possessions, or your own peace and quiet?
- If children are either in danger, or dangerous, do you blame them, or their parents?

2 We are going to look at a cartoon by Posy Simmonds, one of England's best cartoonists, and especially famous for the way she draws and writes about people of different age groups, like children. As you look at the cartoon, do not struggle to understand all the words, but enjoy the drawings, look for the general ideas, and then do the next exercise.

3 In the top picture, the children we see are Victorian, nineteenth-century children. From their clothes, their faces and their games, we can see that at that time people thought children were . . . (finish in not more than ten words).

The adults in the top picture, who are looking at the children playing in the street, think that the parents who allow them to play there are . . . (finish in not more than ten words).

In the bottom picture, the modern, present-day children are

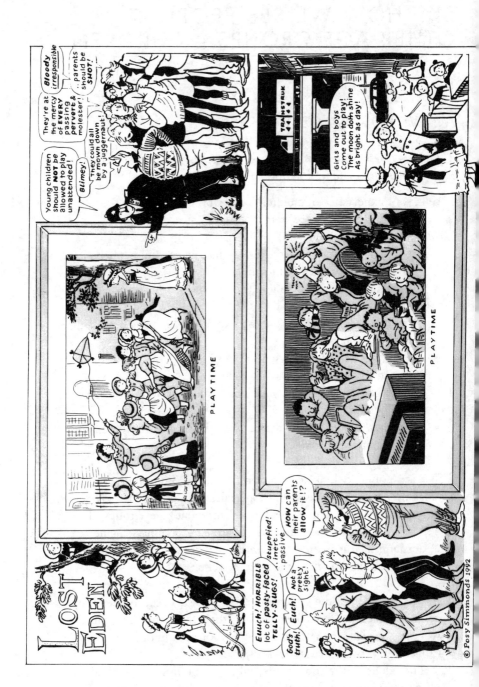

© Posy Simmonds 1992

certainly safe, but now the adults (the same ones we saw in the top picture) think that the children are . . . (finish in not more than ten words), and the parents are . . . (not more than ten words).

In answering these questions, use words that *you* know. Do not repeat words from the cartoon.

ACTIVITIES - STAGE 2:

1 In a cartoon like this, it sometimes matters more, for a language-learner, that you get the general ideas and can express what you feel about the pictures, than that you try to understand and learn every word. For example, if you look at the group of adults in the top picture, you can tell from their bodies and faces what they are feeling. In the list below, circle the words that describe how they feel:

indifferent	*concerned*	*understanding*	*worried*
disapproving	*cold-hearted*	*delighted*	*patient*

Now look at the adults in the bottom picture, and circle the words that describe them:

uninterested	*puzzled*	*sickened*	*detached*
horrified	*disgusted*	*hungry*	*amused*

ACTIVITIES - STAGE 3:

1 Now we are going to look at another view of children by another English cartoonist, Carl Giles, always known simply as Giles. This is a cartoon he did for a National Safety Campaign. But *before* you turn the page and look at it, please do this:

Imagine a group of children left alone in a large kitchen. Think about some of the dangers there, some of the things that children do when left alone.

2 Make a list of the dangers. Simply use *nouns* for these – do not try to write whole sentences. Example: *fire*

3 Now turn the page and look at the cartoon. How many of your dangers did you find in the picture? What are some of the dangers in the picture that you did not have on your list?

ACTIVITIES – STAGE 4:

1 One of the most difficult areas of language for the learner, and one of the most important, is to describe the age group to which certain people belong, and to do this politely, fairly, and without showing prejudice. (We discussed this in Chapter Four, and earlier in this chapter).

Even familiar words like *children* and *old* can be offensive, and the words *boy* and *girl* need very careful use in present-day English. First, take those four words just mentioned, and write beside them the actual ages, in numbers, which you think these words describe. Example: *children* . . . 1–12 (You may not agree!)

2 Now look at some of these words and expressions, and try to put numbers beside them, too. Then compare your answers with other people in the class, and try to decide what the answers reveal about *us*, as well as what the words actually mean in English.

middle-aged	*a man/woman in his/her prime*
getting on a bit	*young adult*
a woman of a certain age	*youngster*
tot	*adolescent*
toddler	*mid-life*
elderly	*kids*
juvenile	*past it*
senior citizen	*wet behind the ears*
a youth	

3 Now, working as a whole class with your teacher, put an E beside the words or phrases which are everyday English, acceptable even in formal writing, and an S beside those which are the kind of slang we can only use in conversation with people we know well.

ACTIVITIES – STAGE 5:

1 Look back at the Giles cartoon. You are going to leave the children alone in the kitchen. Try to prevent accidents, give them some orders about what to do and what not to do. Use **imperatives** for this. Example: *Be careful.*

2 Compare your answers with other people's, in pairs or groups. Your teacher will put some of them up on the board.

3 Why do we often use this form of language, the imperative, when talking to children? What are other situations in which people use imperatives?

When you have answered these two questions, and discussed them in the class, look at some of the examples of imperatives below. We have just said that imperatives are often used for giving orders. However, this is not their only use. Are the examples below orders? If not, write in the column beside them what their real **function** is, what they are doing. The first answer has been filled in to give you an example.

Look out!   (Warning)
                                                      _____

Come in and have a drink.   _____

Don't miss seeing the Houses of Parliament!   _____

Add the onions, and cook gently for
ten minutes.   _____

Deliver us from evil.   _____

4 At your stage of language-learning, you have realized that in the English language the name given to a particular **form** – imperative, present tense – often has very little to do with its real function.

There are good, complete grammar books now which explain all this in detail. In this short book, all we hope to do is to get you to think about and *enjoy* some of the absurdities of the names given to English grammar forms, rather than being bothered or angered by them.

Complete the following sentence, to summarize this stage of the lesson:

Although *be careful* is called an imperative, this form of language can actually be used for many purposes, such as ... and even including ... which is usually addressed to God, to whom few people like to give orders.

SEVEN: HOW WE SEE PEOPLE OF OTHER AGE GROUPS – TEENAGERS

ACTIVITIES – STAGE 1:

1 In the last section we worked with some of the language people use to, and about, children. In this one, we are going to think more about what happens as they grow up. Before we read, first ask yourself, and then discuss as you did in the last section, these questions:

- In your country, do people in general think teenagers are:
  - interesting and lively and attractive
  - promising, giving hope for the future of the country
  - horrible, likely to ruin the country
  - completely selfish
  - something else?
- Compare your own opinion with what you think is the general opinion. How is your opinion affected by your own present age – whether you are in or near this age group, or whether you have to deal with it in some way?

I hate both of you and you hate both of me!

2 Now you are going to read two texts by Alison Lurie, an American writer. The first comes from a novel called *Love and Friendship*. Like many of her books, it is set in an American university town. A young professor and his wife are going to dinner with another professor and his wife, whom they have just recently met.

As you read, try to write down some *adjectives* to describe the family whom Holman and Emily are getting to know for the first time, and their house. In the text, Alison Lurie gives you one adjective, *disorganized*.

3 Also, as you read, check (✓) the statements below which you think are true, and put an ✗ by those you think are false.

(a) Charles, the little boy, makes Holman and Emmy feel welcome and relaxed.
(b) Charles has perfect manners.
(c) Charles is a typical American boy.
(d) Holman treats the little boy, Charles, very nicely.
(e) Hecate, the cat, is not normally allowed in the house.
(f) By the end of the scene, Holman and Emmy are at ease and greatly looking forward to the dinner party.

'What time is it?' Emmy asked as they turned into the street where the Fenns lived.
'Quarter past.'
'We're late.' Emmy was not naturally punctual, but she knew the rules; five or ten minutes past the arranged hour would have been right, but more was too much. She jumped out of the car as soon as it stopped and started up the unshovelled path. Holman followed her.
They stood on the porch and rang the bell, but nobody came.
'Do you suppose it's out of order?' Emmy said.
'Who knows?' Holman looked around him. The Fenns' front porch was very large, but it was in bad repair. The floor was warped, the paint scaling, and the railings broken in several places. Nothing could be seen through the windows, which were covered with cracked yellow shades. 'We could knock.'
He knocked, and so did Emmy, but without result. Instead, from the inside there was the noise of something heavy falling and crashing, and a man's voice shouted: 'God damn it to bloody hell!'

20   Holman and Emmy looked at each other to determine that each had heard this. At this moment the door opened. A thin, peculiar-looking little boy about six years old, in a dirty bathrobe, stood there.

'How do you do?' he said.

25   'We've come to dinner,' said Emmy. 'Are your father and mother in?'

'Yes. Come in, please.' He led them into a large empty hall, lit by one dim bulb in a dusty chandelier. Rooms opened off it, but nobody was visible in any of them. Somewhere above another

30   child could be heard crying. 'It would have been more polite if one of you had said how do you do back,' the boy told them.

'Well, I can make up for that,' Holman said. 'How do you do?'

'Very well, thank you. Who are you? I'm Charles Stephen Zorro Fenn.'

35   'Very pleased to meet you,' Holman said. 'I am Holman Turner and this is my wife Emily.'

'How do you do?'

'How do you do?'

'How do you do?'

40   'Charles!' a woman's voice called from above. 'Come here at once. You let Hecate in again, and now she's made a mess on Katie's bed! Charles, did you hear me?'

'Yes, Mommy. Mommy, Mr Turner is here with his wife Emily.'

There were confused noises. The crying continued. Then steps

45   on the stairs, and Miranda Fenn ran down into the hall. She was wearing a long green velvet dress hung with ropes of jet, but no shoes or stockings. Under one arm and by the scruff of its neck she carried a large black and white cat which was squirming and scratching. 'Oh, excuse me,' Miranda said hurrying past the

50   Turners to the front door. She opened it and threw the cat out. 'I'm terribly sorry,' she said. 'our cat has been sick lately. Julian!' she screamed in quite a different voice. 'Everything seems to be a little disorganized tonight,' she went on. 'But please come in.'

Alison Lurie,
Love and Friendship

ACTIVITIES – STAGE 2:

1 You will notice in this scene that even native English speakers – like the little boy, Charles – find it quite hard to learn the way a polite English conversation with a person you have just met begins and goes on.

By now you know that 'How do you do?' is a question that is simply repeated, not answered. But what is sometimes difficult is carrying the conversation on from there. *Someone* must say something more, or the conversation gets stuck and cannot move forward (as you see in the text!).

Taking the situation outlined below, write an eight-line dialogue between a guest arriving, and his host or hostess.

> Guest and host/hostess have never met before. (Either one can be a man or a woman, as you choose.) The guest is late – the train was delayed. The guest arrives wearing evening clothes. The host/hostess is in jeans and a T-shirt.

GUEST (*as door opens*): How do you do?

2 Now you are going to read another text by the same writer, Alison Lurie. It comes from a novel called *The War Between the Tates*. As you read, try to make three notes about the way the Tate children look; only their *looks*, not their character.

Then look at this group of adjectives that describe traits of character. Put them into two lists, those which do and those which do not accurately describe the Tate children.

polite	*punctual*	*considerate*
choosy	*ill-tempered*	*fussy*
sensitive	*slovenly*	*courteous*
self-centered	*communicative*	*withdrawn*
enthusiastic	*tidy*	*well-groomed*
graceful	*grateful*	*warm*
cheerful	*mature*	*childish*

March 20. A cold spring morning. It rained last night, perforating the crusted snow of the Tates' front lawn, and everything is wet and glitters; the fine gravel of the drive, the ice in the ditch beside it, the bare elm twigs outside the bathroom window. The sun shines
5 sideways at the house, brilliantly, impartially. Seeing it through the kitchen window when she comes down to make breakfast, Erica Tate feels her emotional temperature, which has been unnaturally low of late, rise several degrees.

'Tomorrow's the beginning of spring,' she says to Jeffrey Tate,
10 aged fifteen, as he stumbles into the room fastening his shirt.

'What's for breakfast?'

'Eggs, toast, jam–'

'Any sausages?'

'No, not today.' Erica tries to keep her voice cheerful.

15 'There's never anything to eat in this house,' Jeffrey complains, falling heavily into his chair.

Suppressing several possible answers to this remark, Erica sets a plate before her son and turns towards the stairs, 'Matilda! It's twenty minutes to eight'.

20 'All right! I heard you the first time.'

'Look at that sun,' Erica says to her daughter a few minutes later. 'Tomorrow's the first day of spring.'

No reply. Erica sets a plate in front of Matilda, who will be thirteen next month.

25 'I can't eat this stuff. It's fattening.'

'It's not fattening, it's just an ordinary breakfast, eggs, toast – Anyhow, you're not fat.'

'Everything has gobs of butter on it. It's all soaked in grease.'

'Aw, shut up, Muffy, you'll make me barf.'

30 Again Erica suppresses several rejoinders. 'Would you like me to make you a piece of toast without butter?' she asks rather thinly.

'Okay. If you can do it fast.'

The sun continues to shine into the kitchen. Standing by the toaster, Erica contemplates her children, whom she once thought
35 the most beautiful beings on earth. Jeffrey's streaked blond hair hangs tangled and unwashed over his eyes in front and his collar in back; he hunches awkwardly above the table, cramming fried egg into his mouth and chewing noisily. Matilda, who is wearing a peevish expression and an orange tie-dyed jersey which looks as if
40 it had been spat on, is stripping the crusts off her toast with her fingers. Chomp, crunch, scratch.

The noises sound loud in Erica's head; louder still, as if amplified: CHOMP, CRUNCH, SCRATCH – No. That is coming from outside. She goes to the window. In the field beyond the orchard something yellow is moving. 45

'Hey, the bulldozer's back,' Jeffrey exclaims.

'I guess they're going to put up another ranch-house,' his sister says.

The tone of both these remarks is neutral, even conversational; yet they strike Erica as more coarse and cold than anything that 50 has yet been said this morning. 'You don't care what's happening to our road!' she cries. 'How can you be so selfish, so unfeeling? You don't really mind at all, either of you!'

Her children go on eating. It is evident that they do not.

Chomp; smash. The hands of the clock over the sink move 55 towards eight. Jeffrey and Matilda rise, grumbling, grab their coats and books, and leave to catch the bus for junior high.

Alison Lurie,
The War Between the Tates

ACTIVITIES – STAGE 3:

1 Here are some ways to work out the meaning of the vocabulary in the text from the context in which it is used.

Since the snow outside the house was *crusted*, and the rain *perforated*, it, *crusted* must mean *hard/soft*, and therefore *perforate* must mean to make _____ in something.

Since Erica does not answer Jeffrey when he says 'There's never anything to eat in this house,' *suppressing*, here, must mean not _____.

From what we know of the Tate children's characters, we guess that the *peevish* expression Matilda wears is probably a/an _____ look.

Similarly, from what we know of Jeffrey, we suspect that when he *hunches* awkwardly, he is not _____ up _____.

List any other words you don't know, and try to work out their meaning in similar ways.

2 *Chomp, crunch, scratch.* These words come from the huge vocabulary in which the words actually imitate the sound they are describing. (The English word for this is **onomatopoeia.**)

Some, though not all, of these words come from the noises made by birds, animals and other living creatures. For example, a lion *roars* – we then use the same word to describe the sound of heavy traffic. Look at the drawing below. What sound word would you use when talking about it, to describe the noise that bees make? Where else could you use this word to describe a sound which is nothing to do with bees?

Try now, working in pairs, each to draw something which makes a sound that is represented by words like these. Show your picture to your partner, who will try to guess the word, and will then do the same to you. Your picture can be of anything that makes a noise – not just animals and birds.

Your teacher will put some of these words on the board, so that you can make a list.

Now, to help you to remember some of these words, look first at the picture below. Then, close your eyes. Imagine you are

trying to go to sleep in a hotel room in the centre of a large, noisy city. With your eyes closed, tell your partner some of the sounds you hear, and what causes them.

3 In the first of the two texts in this chapter we met a child, in the second a pair of teenagers. First, try to picture the little boy in the first text, Charles, as he becomes a teenager. Is he like Jeffrey? What does he like to spend his time doing? Is he nice or unpleasant?

Second, try to summarize some of the changes that happen to people as they change from children to teenagers. Use some of the headings below to organize your work. You may want to use some of these **verbs** in your answers: *become, develop, widen, expect, threaten, fear, distrust, experience, hope.*

– their bodies
– their interests
– their relations with one another
– their relations with their parents
– what is expected of them at school
– their feelings about the future

4 Finally, so that we end feeling we have been fair to teenagers, please write one brief paragraph in which you see things from the point of view of either Jeffrey or Matilda. The paragraph can do any of these:

– tell the story of the morning as you saw it – how you felt when you woke up, the breakfast, your mother's way of speaking, your brother or sister
– tell of something that happened the night before, to explain why you felt so horrible the next morning
– tell of something really nice that happened to you recently, when you felt happy and pleased with yourself and the world.

EIGHT: WHAT LANGUAGE CAN TELL ABOUT US AND OTHER PEOPLE

ACTIVITIES – STAGE 1:

1 The language that people use sometimes reveals more about themselves and their situations than they intend. Look at the examples below of people who may do this. Discuss with a partner why this may happen to them, and what their language may reveal. You may think of other examples you want to add.

   – a politician
   – someone trying to sell you something
   – a man persuading a woman to come to his flat
   – a man or woman applying for a job
   – someone wanting you to invest in a business
   – a father explaining why he can't look after the children today

2 Now we are going to read a story from a London newspaper, *The Independent*. The reporter who wrote the story was invited to a party to celebrate the publication of a new book. Imagine that you are the reporter, and write down, before you read, some of the questions you think he will want to have answered at the party.

   These will probably be questions in the present or simple past tenses. They will probably begin with what are called *Wh-* words, like this:
   Who . . .
   What . . .
   When . . .
   Why . . .
   How . . . (Oddly, *How* is called a *Wh-* word!)
   Before you write your questions, you may want to look back at the work we did on word order in Chapter Two (page 12). Word order is, of course, one of the ways in which questions are sometimes different from statements in English. The other is the use of auxiliaries (words like *do* or *did*) and where they come in the question. Now, if you are unsure about anything to do with the grammar of questions in English, ask your teacher. When you

have written your own questions, please add to them this one question from us, which you will find easy to answer when you have read the story: What does Ivana Trump's language reveal?

3 Before you begin to read, looking for answers to your questions, your teacher will tell you how long you have – probably not more than three minutes. Remember that when we read a newspaper story, we don't attempt to understand every word. We only want to know what happened. Now – read fast, look for answers, and try to *enjoy* the story.

'It's a vunderful, vunderful book'

The noisily divorced Ivana Trump has just hatched her first novel, writes Richard Guilliatt

In a Manhattan book store three blocks from her penthouse home, Ivana Trump sits at a table between her mother and her personal assistant, signing autographs. America's foremost divorcee   5
socialite is wearing a grey dress with padded shoulders, a lot of pearls and a remodelled face courtesy of a Californian cosmetic surgeon. Behind her is a wall-sized rack of hard-cover novels bearing her name and the title *For Love Alone*; before her, a queue of fans stretches out the door and down Fifth Avenue.   10

The fans step forward with names printed on slips of paper, a procedure that helps overcome Czech-born Ms Trump's fragile grasp of English. Confronted by a difficult name, she consults her assistant who spells it out in block letters on a notepad. Ms Trump faithfully transcribes the name on the novel's title-page, flashes a   15
smile even brighter than the 10-carat diamond on her left hand and says: 'Sank you. I appreciate very mush.'

No one questions how such a syntactically impaired woman could write a 523-page novel, but then no one wants to cast a shadow over Ms Trump's re-emergence from her ignominious   20
divorce to lapsed billionaire Donald Trump. Armed with $10m, a million-dollar book contract, a $4m mansion and an annual $650,000 in child support and alimony, Ms Trump has transformed herself from affluent trophy wife to Wronged Woman for the Nineties.   25

Although *For Love Alone* bears Ms Trump's name and photograph, few in publishing believe she spent much time writing it. The idea for the book was hatched three years ago in the New York office of Robert Gottlieb, the agent whose previous

30 contribution to literature includes *Scarlett*, sequel to *Gone with the Wind*. Having secured Ms Trump as a client, Mr Gottlieb began selling the idea to publishers in 1990 during the Trumps' very public separation. Pocket Books won the bidding with a reported $1m for two novels.

35 Ms Trump thought up the basic plot of *For Love Alone*. In the book, beautiful Czech model Katrinka Kovar marries wealthy New York property developer Adam Graham and they become 'the golden couple' of the Eighties until he runs off with a floozy, goes broke and divorces her.

40 Finding a writer proved more difficult, for Ms Trump evidently had strict demands. Lucianne Goldberg, the ghostwriter who helped White House wife Maureen Dean with her fictional debut, claims she was offered $350,000 to do *For Love Alone* but turned it down after demanding a 50–50 split. Manhattan writer Liz

45 Nickles says she was fired after Ms Trump accused her of talking to the media. 'It was obvious English was not her first language,' Ms Nickles told *New York Newsday*.

What sets Ms Trump apart is her limited linguistic ability, which is so marked that she needs assistance just to autograph a book,

50 let alone write one. Her avant-garde grammar is a highlight of her interviews. 'I have yesterday the first fan mail,' she tells one television interviewer. 'It's a vunderful, vunderful book!' she gushed to *People*. 'To my surprise I find out I have a great imagination.'

Richard Guilliatt,
The Independent
13 April 1992

ACTIVITIES – STAGE 2:

1 Find four words or phrases in the text which say something about Ivana Trump's English.

2 Obviously, the reporter would not make jokes about her English – and we would not include the text in a book for students! – unless there was something about the situation which made important the fact that her English is not good. Why is her English an important part of the story?

3 Look quickly back through the text, and make brief notes on these subjects (do not write whole sentences, just words or phrases):

- her marriage to Donald Trump
- her present financial situation
- the three main characters in the book
- what happens to the man in the book.

4 Her book is called *For Love Alone*. What do you think of the title?

ACTIVITIES – STAGE 3:

1 The reporter in the story has good fun with Ivana Trump and her language. But does the language he uses tell you anything about him? We know from his name that he is a man, but nothing else about him. We can, however, make guesses. Simply from the words he uses and the way he puts them together, guess which of these statements is likely to be true (we will be guessing too, for we don't know the answers!):

- he is a very elderly and famous writer
- he was foreign-born, and had to learn English himself
- he taught English to foreign students at some time in his life
- he is interested in money and what it can buy
- he admires Ivana Trump's taste in clothes
- he has never heard of the kind of PC language we looked at in Chapter Four
- he probably came to the party wearing an Italian designer suit and a jewelled watch
- he greatly respects the many fans who came to have their books signed
- he enjoyed reading *For Love Alone*.

2 Look at some of the words and phrases below, from the text, and then at the definitions beside them. Put a C if you think the definition is correct, an O if you think it means nearly the opposite to the correct definition.

Floozy: a woman of very strict moral character

Syntactically   a woman whose grammar is so bad it is like a
impaired   disability
woman:

Lapsed   a man with a billion dollars which he has recently
billionaire: increased

Affluent   beautiful wife a rich man marries to display in
trophy   public, like something he has won in a game
wife:

ACTIVITIES – STAGE 4:

1 To end this chapter, and this Unit, we want you to reflect on some of the grammar which you understood and used throughout this part of the book, although we didn't draw your attention to it. We will then ask you to think about it in more detail. To begin, look very quickly at the first paragraph of the news story you have just read, about Ivana Trump. What are the two tenses used in this paragraph?

2 Now look, also very quickly, at the second of the two texts by Alison Lurie, the one from *The War Between the Tates* on page 48. In the first few paragraphs, do you find all *past* tenses?

3 Quite clearly, both of these two texts are telling the reader something that happened in the past. Yet both of them use present tenses (the present simple, the present continuous, or both). Why do these two skilled writers introduce these present tenses? What effect do they have on the reader?

4 Here are a few examples from this Unit of the ways in which we use present tenses.

Chapter One: giving personal details about yourself, your
                  interests, your situation.

Chapter Two: describing other people – their appearance, clothes, character.

Chapter Three: telling the doctor what is wrong with you.

Chapter Four: describing and identifying groups of people.

You will find present tenses both in some of the texts in these and other chapters, and in the work we asked you to do on the texts. (There are, of course, many other tenses used in some of the texts.)

5 Rather than following the more traditional approaches to grammar, we would like you now to draw on what you already know, and what you have been doing in this Unit, to revise and reinforce your sense of what the present tenses can do.

6 By now, at your advanced stage of learning English, you have realized that the names of English tenses, like many other grammar terms in English (the imperative, for instance) have little to do with the real function of the tenses.

You know, of course, the usual difference in meaning between these two sentences:

I live in Brussels.   I'm living in Brussels.

Next year – Rome . . .

Brussels

But these two uses are only a small part of the story of these two tenses. To help you recall what you know already, and perhaps to extend your knowledge, here is an exercise to end this Unit.

Below are some functions (some ways of using these tenses). Please choose the ones which are possible for each of the two present tenses, write them under the name, and then give an example of each. Some functions are possible for both tenses.

> *Functions:*
> an action planned for the future
> an action happening at the moment of speaking
> a habitual or permanent action or state
> a temporary action or state, not necessarily happening at the moment of speaking
> an action in the past, which the writer wants you to feel is happening now
> a habitual action about which the speaker has powerful feelings
> can you add any other functions?

PRESENT SIMPLE		PRESENT CONTINUOUS	
Functions:	*Examples:*	*Functions:*	*Examples:*

UNIT II

ONE: UNDERSTANDING YOUR OWN COUNTRY

ACTIVITIES – STAGE 1:

1 Close your eyes and think of your own country. Now open them. What picture came into your head? Was it of something happening now, something famous that happened in the past, or something that will happen in the future? Did you feel happy and proud, or did you feel worried and uncertain? Talk first to your partner, comparing your thoughts. Then report your thoughts to the class.

2 Look now at this cartoon. It was drawn by one of England's most famous cartoonists, whose real name was Graham Laidler, but who was always known as Pont. He lived from 1908–40. This cartoon comes from a famous series called The British Character. People we know who have looked at the cartoon agree with us that the man's clothes, hairstyle, and the room could be found unchanged in England in the 1990s.

THE BRITISH CHARACTER.
A TENDENCY TO THINK THINGS NOT SO GOOD AS THEY USED TO BE.

3 When you have looked at the cartoon, choose the correct ending for each of these sentences.

- the man in the picture is: (a) sad (b) angry (c) ill.
- the newspaper has been: (a) blown across the room by a strong wind (b) thrown to a friend we can't see in the picture (c) thrown away because the man is furious at something he has just read.
- what he was reading in the newspaper was probably about (a) something happening now that he dislikes (b) a country he hopes to visit (c) good news about his favourite football team.

4 The words under the picture could be understood to mean (choose the correct summary):

(a) the British, in general, dislike reading newspapers and prefer more up-to-date news on radio and television
(b) older British people have more character than younger ones, because they have seen more of life
(c) British people prefer the past to the present.

ACTIVITIES – STAGE **2**:

1 Now you are going to read a text by Keith Waterhouse, a journalist, novelist, playwright and film writer. This is one of a series of regular columns he writes for the popular newspaper the *Daily Mail*. As you read, try to decide whether Keith Waterhouse is typical of the British tendency to think things not so good as they used to be, or whether he is an exception to the rule. Circle the correct answer:

    He is typical   He is an exception

2 You will probably find many examples in the text to support your answer. Try to choose the one example that you think is the strongest proof of what you think.

Moving addresses

Among the augurs indicating that there have been rosier periods of history to live in than the last quarter of the 20th century is the fact that everywhere these days is somewhere else.

You may have noticed this. Say you fall off your bicycle and hobble round to your local hospital. You may depend upon it that you will find a big sign advising that there is no casualty department and recommending that you try another hospital on the other side of town.

Check before you do this. It is probably now an old people's home, to accommodate the folk who were in the almshouses until they were pulled down to make way for a new supermarket which replaces the one that used to be in the High Street before it became a home computer centre.

The library is in the old town hall. The town hall staff are in the new civic centre, except for the planning department which is in the old library.

Do not look for the vicar in the vicarage. The vicarage, now known as the Old Vicarage, houses only a retired civil servant, who writes letters to *The Times*. The vicar is in the new vicarage which is on the site of the old police station. The new police station is on the site of the old brewery.

Few things are certain in this age of anxiety, but of one thing you may be absolutely sure. If you pass an old building that looks like a school, and which has the legend 'School' hewn into the stone, you may take it that it is no longer a school but a used furniture depository.

You think I exaggerate? Then look over my shoulder at the newspaper clipping on my desk. It announces that the Greenwich Observatory is to be moved from Herstmonceux Castle in West Sussex to Cambridge University (which at the moment of writing remains in Cambridge).

These cannot be good times to be a postman.

Everywhere being somewhere else seems exclusively a British convention. If you go to France or Italy or even to America, with its not entirely deserved reputation for demolishing buildings almost before they are finished, you will find, by and large, that the school is in the schoolhouse, the fire brigade in the fire station and the mayor in his parlour, and that even if all's not well in the world, at least you know where it is.

Labour councils, with a few allegedly go-ahead Tory ones

thrown in, are mainly responsible for turning the country into a gigantic game of chess, where every institution, as well as much of the population, has to keep moving to another square. In the great municipal boom of the Sixties and early Seventies, they nurtured
5   the extravagant belief that any old building must have outlived its use, that only spanking new premises custom-built to contain the white heat of technology were good enough.

This thought process, if that's what you want to call it, is now ingrained. And so even though the money earmarked to pull
50   England down and start again has now run out, there is still this constant urge to re-locate everyone from the 'unsuitable' accommodation they have endured for a hundred or two hundred years usually to somewhere nastier.

I've half a mind to write to the Prime Minister about it. Is she still
55   at No. 10 Downing Street, does anyone happen to know?

Keith Waterhouse,
Daily Mail
Monday, November 17, 1986

ACTIVITIES – STAGE 3:

1 Generally, Keith Waterhouse, writing in a popular newspaper, uses simple words you will know. The few more unusual words in the text are easy to guess from their context. Match the words on the left with the definitions on the right.

augurs   walk awkwardly because of an injury

almshouses   a priest in the Church of England

hobble   a house or other building

vicar   a building in which scientists observe the stars

observatory   put aside for a special purpose

ingrained   permanent, unlikely to change

earmarked   signs of the future

premises   places specially built many years ago to house old people

2 Here is a list of some of the places mentioned in the text. Put them into two lists. First, list the old kinds of places the writer likes. Then, list the new kinds of places he dislikes.

OLD PLACES HE LIKES	NEW PLACES HE DISLIKES

(a) a local hospital which includes
     a casualty department

(b) a home computer centre

(c) the almshouses

(d) a school building which has a
     sign on it saying *school* and
     which actually is a school.

(e) the planning department of the
     town hall

(f) the Old Vicarage in which a
     retired civil servant lives

(g) the used furniture depository

3 Interestingly, this text which is so much about the past uses a mixture of tenses, mainly the present. But if you wanted to tell someone about what Keith Waterhouse discovered as he walked around the town, you would use the two tenses we mainly employ for this purpose:

– the **simple past,** which students at your level know how to use without difficulty for things that happened in a period clearly separated from the present
– the **past perfect**, which we use when for some reason we don't want to tell the events in the exact order they happened: this tense enables us to say clearly that an event happened before another, even though we tell of it afterwards. Example:

> A man fell off his bicycle. He hobbled around to his local hospital. When he got there, he found they had closed the casualty department.

The events, told in the order they happened, are:

> They closed the casualty department.
> The man fell off his bicycle.
> He hobbled around to the hospital.

The past perfect *had closed* tells the reader that this event happened before the two events in the simple past tense.

Imagine a man like Keith Waterhouse took a walk around his town, and found many changes – all of which, obviously, happened *before* he discovered them. Using the facts in the text, complete these sentences with past perfect tenses, in some cases two of them.

(a) The same man who fell off his bicycle and went to the hospital was told to try another hospital on the other side of town. But when he got there, he found . . .

(b) Some people went to visit their elderly friends in the famous old almshouses. But when they got there, they found that the almshouses . . .

(c) A busy woman went out to do her shopping at the supermarket in the High Street. When she got there, she found that . . .

(d) A couple desperate to get married in a hurry went to the Old Vicarage to see the vicar. But when they got there, they found that the vicar . . .

(e) A man who had been robbed rushed to the old police station to report the crime. When he got there he found . . .

(f) A man who wanted to collect some beer he'd ordered for his restaurant went to the place where the brewery had always been. But when he got there, he found that the brewery . . .

4 Have *you* ever had a shock, when you went to somewhere you knew and liked, and found that it had closed, changed, or otherwise done something to disappoint you? Tell your partner about it, using the correct tenses.

5 Another structure we often need when talking about the past is *used to*. Look back at the words under the cartoon. We use it not only for personal habits we have discontinued ('I used to smoke, but I stopped.') but also for places and national institutions that have changed. Examples:

The vicar used to live in The Old Vicarage, but now he lives in the new one, where the old police station used to be.

The British used to be a nation of tea-drinkers, but now many of them prefer coffee.

Think of some ways in which your own country has changed, and give some examples of this: tell us how things *used to be*, and how they are now.

ACTIVITIES – STAGE 4:

1 Could you find people in your country wearing clothes, and in rooms, which have not changed for fifty years or longer, like the examples in the Pont cartoon? Do you dress as your mother or father did?

2 Waterhouse says of his country, 'These cannot be good times to be a postman.' Is this true of your country?

3 Discuss your answers with your partner. Then, working together, look at the line: 'A tendency to think things not so good as they used to be.' Note the grammar:

A tendency + infinitive

Write, with your partner, a similar line about your own country.

TWO: LOOKING BEYOND YOUR OWN COUNTRY

ACTIVITIES – STAGE 1:

1 Look at the drawing below. Then, very quickly, do a drawing of the group of people you see yourself, most importantly, as belonging to.

2 Compare your drawing with your partner's. Does your group represent your family, your town or village, your country, or some much larger unit – Europe, South America, South-east Asia, Africa?

3 Do you think of yourself mainly as a citizen of your country, or as a part of some larger group which may not be political: religious, racial, or some grouping which is completely international: women, young people, people who wear glasses?

4 Do you think you are likely to change your feelings as you get older – to feel more or less a part of some community, country, or group?

ACTIVITIES – STAGE 2:

1 You are now going to read something written by Mel's elder daughter, Stephanie. She writes for television, magazines, and newspapers – including *The Times*, where this article appeared.

2 Before you read Stephanie Calman's article, look at this summary of what you read in Chapter One.

> Keith Waterhouse is an Englishman of the older generation who is typically British, and who thinks that life was better thirty years ago, when things were simpler, and before so many changes happened, all of which made life worse.

Do you agree with this summary?

3 As you read Stephanie Calman's article, please rewrite the sentence to turn it into an accurate summary of her and her opinions.

> Stephanie Calman is . . .

4 Compare your answer with your partner's. Your teacher will then ask you and the others in your class what you have written, and try to get the class to agree on a summary.

Local body in identity crisis

Are you gearing yourself up for Europe? Are you preparing for entry into the single market? Or, as the posters have it, où will vous be in 1992? I went to a lunch party last week which, if it had not been for the good food and delightful company, would have rendered me completely depressed. Half the guests were Italian.   5
But they were not just Italian, they were European. In fact, a couple of them were downright international. It was not only that they'd lived all over the place and spoke at least three languages; they seemed to think in a non-parochial, global sort of way.
    Most annoyingly, they were not chic, rich, matching-luggage   10
people – the kind for whom the phrase 'economy ticket' is a foreign language. Even the Australian hostess laughed at the Italian jokes, knew how to use basil in a daring way and was generally far more European than I.

15   'Listen mate,' I wanted to say. 'My background is Glaswegian
        and Lithuanian (I nearly said Russian). I was European before I
        was *born*.' But there was no point. I was sure by dusk of what no
        amount of passport stamps and Benetton knitwear could conceal: I
        am and always will be irretrievably local.
20   Having faced my disability, the question is, should I care? Will I
        end up in the care of therapeutic professionals: 'Your cultural
        counsellor will see you now, Ms Calperson,' and as a silhouetted
        figure in documentaries: 'I tried, but I just couldn't stop buying
        English magazines from the bottom shelf,' doomed to think and
25   write in just the one language forever?
        Probably, and so what? I do not feel part of the European
        community, but then I have never felt part of the Great British one
        either.
        For a start, nobody believes I was born here. Every time I go up
30   Oxford Street, I get flyers shoved at me for English language
        courses which I only fail to give straight back again because the
        European students handing them out are not familiar with the
        phrase, 'No thank you, I live here.'
        So I stuff them in the bin, wincing at the waste of paper. (I tried
35   recycling them as shopping lists, but the Greek check-out woman
        at Safeway found one on the conveyor belt and asked me at great
        length if I'd been home to Cyprus this year.)
        As far as I can tell, emotionally it will make little difference
        whether Europe is a single market, an enormous shopping centre
40   (more likely), or a row of stalls up the Goldhawk Road. Most
        people I meet have no idea what it means. Half my London friends,
        after all, are still coping with the trauma of being made 081. But
        that's OK, since we all know we are citizens of One World. Every
        time we buy a sustainable softwood coffee table, we feel really,
45   really aware of the people of the rain-forest.
        When I do not give money to the homeless youths in the
        doorways, I console myself with a warm glow from the parcel of
        soap and stockings I sent to a family of graphic designers in
        Warsaw which, incidentally, was pretty European of me.
50   The reason I do not mind not feeling part of my community is
        that I am somewhat doubtful of the whole notion, not least because
        I'm fed up with being told that, like tomatoes and shop service,
        they were vastly superior before I was born.
        The community, some of my elders would have me believe, is
55   not something which we need to learn about from continentals or
        Amazons, but is a great institution which (like the empire and

home baking) once held the country together and has now crumbled away.

It looked after people who rallied round, pulled together and, oh yes, made their own fun. They did not need youth television, social workers or personal hygiene products in a range of five fragrances. 60

People were so much lovelier to each other, they were practically another species. You knew your neighbour. Oh, really? And did that include newly arrived Commonwealth members, gentlemen who preferred other gentlemen and women who became mothers without managing to be wives first? 65

Now society at large tolerates a wider range of behaviour. But communities still demand a deal of conformity as part of the membership price. At best, this means losing the nice black passport. At worst, it involves giving up those parts of your identity considered too 'odd' for the comfort of everyone else. 70

It is a 'sense of community' which obliges a poor old person to fill endless official charity envelopes rather than face handing them back empty to their friendly local collector. It requires wildlife-loving gardeners to slash rambling hedges because all the others have right angles and, horticulturally, it's cool to be square. It persuades one householder not to paint her front door purple in a row of white in case her neighbours give her the cold shoulder. That's not a community, that's a protection racket. 75

80

Everybody's a bit weird when you come down to it. You might wear a purse on a string round your neck and listen to Richard Clayderman, but that does not mean I can give you a hard time. Besides, in a couple of years' time, it might be all the rage.

Stephanie Calman,
The Times
16 June 1990

ACTIVITIES – STAGE 3:

1 Stephanie Calman's article is a useful example of the way in which a piece of writing is organized. It has a single major theme – which you have already agreed – but develops this by following a number of smaller themes. First, look at the two opening paragraphs, and choose which of the following is the best description of their theme.

(a) A lunch party at which everyone was rich and chic, had matching luggage and cooked with basil.

(b) A lunch party at which the Australian hostess laughed rudely at her guests because they were Italian.

(c) A lunch party where the guests were skilled linguists and seemed more comfortable than Stephanie Calman with the idea of being European.

2 Below are brief descriptions of some of the other smaller themes which the article develops. Please put them into the order in which they appear in the article.

(a) People are individuals, and communities should not force them to conform.

(b) Communities, especially those in the recent past in England, were much more intolerant of black people, gay people, and single mothers than the present generation.

(c) Because one of her parents came from Scotland, and some of her grandparents from Lithuania, Stephanie Calman has never felt really British.

(d) Stephanie Calman is mistaken for a foreigner in England.

(e) Stephanie Calman not only does not feel part of any larger community – even the world – but she is also doubtful of the whole idea of a community.

3 This article explores the relationship between one person, and various groups, starting with smaller ones and moving on to larger ones. Look at the circles, and then at the words and phrases below.

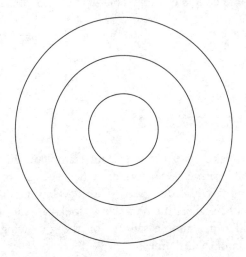

Put into the small circle in the centre the words which are about one person, into the outer circle those which are about the largest group or groups, and into the middle circle those which come in between. The words are a mixture of nouns and adjectives.

non-parochial	*citizens of One World*	*continentals*
global	*community*	*your identity*
European	*the country*	*I*
international	*neighbours*	*local*

ACTIVITIES – STAGE 4:

1 Look at this quotation from the article: 'Now society at large tolerates a wider range of behaviour. But communities still demand a deal of conformity as part of the membership price.'

  Do you agree with this quotation? Is it true of your country, or of the other larger or smaller communities which we have discussed in this chapter?

2 After the class has had time to discuss these questions, please write *one* paragraph only, expressing your opinions on the subject, but relating it specifically to something *you* have experienced. Give specific examples, and write only 100–250 words.

THREE: EXPLORING YOUR OWN COUNTRY

ACTIVITIES – STAGE 1:

1 Read these sentences which come near the beginning of a book we are going to read more of in this section. Try to guess some basic facts about the writer: sex, age, nationality, occupation, present place of residence. Then guess what the book is likely to be about.

On another continent, 4,000 miles away, I became quietly seized with that nostalgia that overcomes you when you have reached the middle of your life and your father has recently died and it dawns on you that when he went he took some of you with him. I wanted to go back to the magic places of my youth – to Mackinac Island, the Rocky Mountains, Gettysburg – and see if they were as good as I remembered them. I wanted to hear the long, low sound of a Rock Island locomotive calling across a still night and the clack of it receding into the distance. I wanted to see lightning bugs, and hear cicadas shrill, and be inescapably immersed in that hot, crazy-making August weather that makes your underwear scoot up every crack and fissure and cling to you like latex, and drives mild-mannered men to pull out hand-guns in bars and light up the night with gunfire. I wanted to look for Ne-Hi Pop and Burma Shave signs and go to a ball game and sit at a marble-topped soda-fountain and drive through the kind of small towns that Deanna Durbin and Mickey Rooney used to inhabit in the movies. I wanted to travel around. I wanted to see America. I wanted to come home.

2 Here is some information about the writer and the book. Compare your answers with your partner's, and then with these facts. Could you have guessed the answers more correctly than you did, or are some of the questions impossible to answer from the few sentences you read?

The author of the book is Bill Bryson, an American married to an English woman and living in England. At the time of writing this book – in 1989 – he was thirty-eight years old. He is a journalist

who has written for *The Times* and *The Independent*. The full title
of the book is *The Lost Continent: Travels in Small Town America*.
Bill Bryson was born in a small town in Iowa, and the book is
about his travels in the lesser-known parts of America.

3 Please discuss these questions with your partner, and then report
your answers.

- Why would a man of Bill Bryson's age want to explore his own
  country, rather than some country he had never seen?
- Look at the words *small town* in the title. What is the difference
  between *small town America*, and big cities like New York,
  Chicago, Miami, Los Angeles? Which would you rather visit?
  Why?

Have you really explored your own country? Did you find any
differences between small places and large ones? Did you get any
surprises?

ACTIVITIES – STAGE 2:

1 Before you read what Bill Bryson discovered in the small town of
Sonora, California, make a few notes, based on your answers to
the questions you have just answered, on what you would *expect*
him to find. Use these headings:

The place he stayed: hotel/motel

The room, the facilities

The place he ate

The person who served him there

2 As you read, make further notes comparing your answers with
what he did find there.

In the evening I drove on to Sonora, through a tranquil sunset,
along sinuous mountain roads. I reached the town after dark and
had difficulty finding a room. It was only the middle of the week,
but most places were full. The motel I finally found was grossly
5   overpriced and the TV reception was terrible. It was like watching
people moving around in front of fun-house mirrors. Their bodies
would proceed across the screen and their heads would follow a
moment later, as if connected by elastic. I was paying $42 for this.
The bed was like a pool table with sheets. And the toilet seat didn't
10   have a 'Sanitized For Your Protection' wrapper on it, denying me
my daily ritual of cutting it with my scissors and saying, 'I now
declare this toilet open.' These things become important to you
when you have been alone on the road for a while. In a sour
mood I drove into town and went to a cheap restaurant for dinner.
15   The waitress made me wait a long time before she came and took
my order. She looked tarty and had an irritating habit of repeating
everything I said to her.
         'I'd like the chicken fried steak,' I said.
         'You'd like the chicken fried steak?'
20   'Yes. And I would like French fries with it.'
         'You want French fries with it?'
         'Yes. And I would like a salad with Thousand Island dressing.'
         'You want a salad with Thousand Island dressing?'
         'Yes, and a Coke to drink.'
25   'You want a Coke to drink?'
         'Excuse me, miss, but I've had a bad day and if you don't stop
repeating everything I say, I'm going to take this ketchup bottle
and squirt it all down the front of your blouse.'
         'You're going to take that ketchup bottle and squirt it all down
30   the front of my blouse?'
         I didn't really threaten her with ketchup – she might have had a
large boy-friend who would come and pummel me; also, I once
knew a waitress who told me that whenever a customer was rude
to her she went out to the kitchen and spat in his food, and since
35   then I have never spoken sharply to a waitress or sent
undercooked food back to the kitchen (because the cook spits in it,
you see) – but I was in such a disagreeable mood that I put my
chewing-gum straight into the ashtray without wrapping it in a
piece of tissue first, as my mother always taught me to do, and

pressed it down with my thumb so that it wouldn't fall out when the 40
ashtray was turned over, but would have to be prised out with a
fork. And what's more – God help me – it gave me a tingle of
satisfaction.

Bill Bryson,
The Lost Continent

ACTIVITIES – STAGE 3:

1 Report to the class on how your guesses compared with what
actually happened in the book.

2 To check, quickly, your understanding of the text, choose the best
of the choices offered on each subject below.

The Town

Empty
Over-populated
Surprisingly crowded

The Motel

Cheap
Expensive
With a sensible pricing system

The bed

Hard
Soft
Equipped with its own special pool table

The TV reception

Perfect
Technically advanced
Distorted

The waitress

Friendly
Efficient
Apparently unintelligent

Bill Bryson's response

Sexually attracted
Angry and revengeful
Indifferent

3 Here are some sentences using words from the book in a different context. Choose the correct words from the text to put into the sentences. In the brackets are some definitions to help you.

His mother didn't like his new girlfriend; she thought the girl was _____ (vulgar, almost like a prostitute).

When the referee stopped the fight, the boxer was still trying to _____ the other man (hit repeatedly).

The door was stuck, so we _____ it open (forced).

4 Now find three words in the text with the meanings below, and put them into sentences of your own.

_____ (very peaceful)

_____ (curving gently)

_____ (a very pleasant feeling in the body)

5 Look at lines 26–28, in which Bill Bryson tells you what he wanted to say, but was afraid to. Have you ever been in such a situation? Write briefly (not more than fifty words) what you wanted to say. Tell the class what the situation was, read what you didn't actually say, and explain why you decided not to say it.

ACTIVITIES – STAGE 4:

1 Imagine that you are offered a long holiday with a car, enough money and enough time to do what you like. You can spend it either: (a) exploring your own country, or (b) exploring either small-town America or its big cities. First, make your choice, and then put it into correct grammatical form, using one of these structures:

I'd much prefer . . . (+ *to* infinitive)

I'd much rather . . . (+ infinitive without *to*)

Given that choice, I'd opt . . . (+ *to* infinitive)

2 Now, to explain your choice, give some details, using some of the possible forms of the structure below (the second conditional):

If I	went to . . .
	visited . . .
	chose to explore . . .
I	would . . .
	would be able to . . .
	could . . .
	might . . .

3 When the class has reported, and you have all heard what other people said, does anyone want to change plans?

FOUR: EXPLORING OTHER COUNTRIES

ACTIVITIES – STAGE 1:

1 Travelling to other countries, not on business but because we want to, is, when you stop to think, a strange activity. We leave the comfort of our homes to be among strangers, to risk discomfort or even danger. Why do we do it? Discuss your own views with your partner, and then see whether the whole class agrees on the subject.

2 Many writers have recently discussed the difference between tourists and travellers. Look at the list below of some of the things people do when they visit other countries, and then put each one under what is, in your opinion, the correct heading.

TRAVELLERS   TOURISTS

        (a) learn some of the
             language of the country so
             that they can speak it to
             people if they meet.
        (b) Travel in a coach full of
             people from their own
             country.

(c) Eat in their hotel food cooked by chefs who know what their hotel guests are used to.

(d) Travel on trains and buses used by local people.

(e) See the famous sights which everyone who goes to that country looks at.

(f) Eat the local food with local people.

(g) Go to places few visitors have seen, even when difficult or uncomfortable.

(h) Meet, talk to, share experiences with local people.

ACTIVITIES – STAGE 2:

1 Now you are going to read a short extract from a book called *Inca-Kola*. It was written by one of England's most interesting young writers, Matthew Parris. Born in Africa, he is a former diplomat and Member of Parliament, now a journalist and television presenter, who writes a regular political column for *The Times*. *Inca-Kola* tells about a trip he made to Peru with three other young men: Mick, John and Ian. Read the text quickly, just to get an impression, and to decide this question: were Matthew Parris and his friends travellers or tourists?

2 Referring back to question 2 in Activities, stage 1, give some reasons for your answer.

It was now that Ian made what seemed at first a most unlucky move.

It started when our bus drove off without one of the passengers.

They had nicknamed him El Gordo (The Fat One). He was a grossly overweight, middle-aged travelling salesman (we never quite worked out in what) whose shabby suit was literally bursting at its seams, and who perspired continuously. He was probably on

5

his third helping of soup as the bus pulled away. *'Falta El Gordo'*
(El Gordo is missing), Ian shouted. Other passengers took up the
cry. *'Falta El Gordo,'* yelled the whole bus.

We shuddered to a halt. Far back, in the dust, El Gordo could
be seen, waddling desperately behind us, calling for us to wait.
He caught up – panting – and heaved himself up the steps, soaked
with sweat, to general laughter.

What happened next seemed so unfair to Ian. El Gordo was
standing at the front of the bus, Ian sitting (with us) in the back
seats. But El Gordo's own seat, which should have been waiting
for him, seemed to have disappeared. This was not surprising.
Ever since our departure from Lima, no one had wanted his huge
bulk next to them because he overflowed hopelessly into
surrounding seats.

But he had eventually established a place next to an Indian
mother. Mothers can be ruthless. She was the dog who hadn't
barked when he failed to board, leaving Ian to announce that he
was missing. She it was who had made a quick use of his absence
and conjured children out of nowhere to fill his seat.

El Gordo lurched, still perspiring, down the gangway, eyeing
every slight gap between passengers. But as fast as he spotted
gaps, passengers moved to close them. 'No! No! El Gordo no!'
they chanted. The women shrieked with laughter as The Fat One
ran the gauntlet of their inhospitality, row by row. Moving down
from the front of the bus, still searching, he neared the back.

A look of alarm grew on Ian's face as the inevitable became
clear. He was at the very back, the terminus of El Gordo's
hopeless search. And there was a tiny space just next to him. As
relief spread across El Gordo's plump features, there was horror in
Ian's eyes.

Into the gap crashed El Gordo, shirt dripping. Did the offending
hulk realize that it was his saviour whom he now almost crushed?
Probably not. Ian groaned. The whole bus grinned.

We lurched forward again, on into the darkness. One by one,
each of us fell asleep. El Gordo snored peacefully; the woman
who had evicted him was comfortable now, her children around
her. Señora Fernandez had stopped crying and was calm. Mick
and John dozed. Even Ian drifted off, as one pinned helplessly
underground in a mining disaster might drift from consciousness.

That we started to climb, and climbed continuously until dawn, we
knew more as you know it on an aeroplane than on a bus. We

could see almost nothing outside; but it was easy to tell that the
road was winding up the side of the Andes. Through a fitful sleep   50
we were conscious of the whole dead weight of the bus heaving
regularly, left to right, then back again. The springs creaked and
the luggage piled on the roof above shifted heavily. The moon
swung wildly across the windows as we hairpinned upwards – not
for ten minutes as in Scotland, or twenty as in Switzerland: but for   55
the whole of the rest of the night . . . left, right, left . . .

The slope of the bus floor, steeply uphill, stayed constant while
the stars outside spun crazily in the sky. From time to time a child
cried, but mostly there was silence, and darkness without. Little
clusters of lights down on the coast, now so far below us, were   60
sometimes visible, and the spines of mountain ridges showed white
and skeletal in the moonlight, like the bones of hands reaching
down towards them. We seemed to be climbing through thin air.

Once the bus stopped, rather before dawn. When we got to our
feet to stretch our legs, we found ourselves breathing hard in the   65
rarefied atmosphere.

It was getting very cold. The bus had no heating at all. All
around us the peasants produced blankets, ponchos and shawls –
from nowhere, it seemed, as conjurors produce silk scarves – and
disappeared beneath them. The windows, already misted over,   70
froze on the inside.

John shivered and felt sick. Mick's feet were so cold that he put
all his socks on, planted his legs in a plastic bag, then placed the
whole bundle into a travelling bag. This completely immobilized
him.   75

It was then that we noticed Ian. No longer recoiling from El
Gordo he had now snuggled right up close, almost enveloped by
one fatty flank. El Gordo himself, a warm, slumbering mound,
heaved rhythmically with gentle snores. Alone among us, Ian was
warm, his face a picture of peaceful repose. Virtue had had its   80
reward.

Matthew Parris,
Inca-Kola

ACTIVITIES – STAGE 3:

1 Now read the text again, more carefully. This is a story with what
is called in English a **moral** – a general truth which the story
illustrates. The moral is, in this story, the last sentence: *Virtue had
had its reward.*

Put in simpler words, what does this mean? Choose the best sentence.

(a) The world we live in is a tough place, and only those who look after their own interests can expect any reward.
(b) A good action, done for unselfish reasons, in this case produced an unexpectedly good result.
(c) Those who behave well are rewarded in heaven for their actions, even though they may suffer on earth.

2 Check your understanding further by choosing the correct ending.

Virtue is . . .

good, unselfish behaviour
an illness
extreme cold

Therefore a virtuous person is . . .

a good person
a sick person
a cold person

The virtuous person in this story is . . .

El Gordo
Ian
The Indian mother

His/her virtuous action was . . .

eating the third helping of soup
making the bus wait for a late passenger
filling the empty seat with children

3 Finally, draw a simple picture of the two main characters in the story, as they appear in the last paragraph of the text.

ACTIVITIES – STAGE **4**:

1 In Chapter One of this Unit we looked at the way in which the past perfect tense is used, always in the context of some uses of the simple past, to make clear the *order* of events. This text from *Inca-Kola* uses the past perfect many times for this purpose. For example (line 22) 'But he had eventually established a place next to an Indian mother.' To be certain that you have understood how these tenses work, place the events in the story in the order in which they *happened* rather than the order in which they are told.

The weather became very cold.

The passengers named the man El Gordo.

El Gordo ate a third helping of soup.

The Indian mother put her children into El Gordo's seat.

Ian was the only warm person on the bus.

The bus climbed high into the mountains.

El Gordo sat by Ian.

El Gordo could not sit where he first sat.

Ian shouted for the bus to stop.

El Gordo found a seat next to the Indian mother.

No one wanted El Gordo to sit by them.

2 In a well-told story, one event often causes another to happen rather than simply happening first. We often link such events by words like *because, so, as a result, consequently*. Examples:

Because they were high in the mountains, the bus got cold.

Consequently, peasants took out blankets to keep warm.

Mick's feet were cold, so he put all his socks on, put his legs in a plastic bag, and then inside his travelling bag.

As a result, he couldn't move.

Look back now at the events of the story, which you have put into correct order. Some, though *not all* of these events happen as a result of some event before. Try to link some of the sentences by using some of the words like *because*.

3 When events in the past are linked as they are in this story, we can look back at them and guess how things might have happened differently. For this purpose we often use the structure called the third conditional. Example:

If Matthew Parris hadn't travelled to Peru, he wouldn't have met El Gordo and the other people on the bus.

Before you go on to the next exercise, your teacher may want to review the grammar of the third conditional with you.

4 The story Matthew Parris tells is how Ian did something good, and as a result something good happened to him.

Using the third conditional, imagine that Ian did not do this good action, and then what followed.

Look at some of the other events, and see which ones of them could have happened differently. Give some examples of these – two or three only – using the third conditional.

ACTIVITIES – STAGE 5:

1 When you read a story like this one, does it make you want to travel to a far-off country, or to stay comfortably at home?

2 Why?

FIVE: ENCOUNTERING PEOPLE FROM YOUR OWN COUNTRY ABROAD

ACTIVITIES – STAGE 1:

1 You know from the first chapter of this book that one of its authors, Ben, is an American who lives in England, and that Mel, as a journalist, often travels abroad to America and other countries. So we often come across people from our own country when they are travelling abroad, and therefore see them through the eyes of people from other countries. Have you had this experience? Have you watched your own fellow-countrymen and countrywomen, seen how they behaved as travellers (and tourists)? How did you feel about them? Were you proud or ashamed? Did they make you realize things about yourself you hadn't noticed before? Did they help you to understand yourself better?

2 We are now going to read two short scenes from a recent play, *Some Americans Abroad*, by Richard Nelson. Remember that when we read a play, we must understand from the dialogue what people are thinking and feeling – they do not always tell us things directly.

You will find in the text the word *Beat*. This is to tell the actors to pause, like an instruction in a piece of music. In these two scenes we meet Joe Taylor, an American professor of English, and Joanne, an American woman married to an English man. Joe is taking a group of American students on a tour of England, including visits to the theatre. Joanne, as part of her work, books the seats for these visits. The first scene happens in a part of the Royal National Theatre, in London, the second at the Royal Shakespeare Theatre in Shakespeare's birthplace, Stratford-upon-Avon.

As you read, look at the list of words below. Put into one group (under their names) the words you think describe how Joe and Joanne see themselves, and in the other how they see Americans they meet in England.

| JOE AND JOANNE | OTHER AMERICANS ABROAD |

well-educated

over-friendly

loud

tasteful

refined

brash

crude

well-dressed

sophisticated

vulgar

tourists

travellers

Your teacher may ask you to check the meaning of any word you do not know, before you start.

Please also, as you work, fill in the missing words in these sentences. You will probably not find the actual words in the text. You must look for the information there, but use words of your own to report.

When Joe and Joanne meet other Americans in England, they feel _____, and hope that the Americans will not _____ that Joe and Joanne are Americans, too. Joanne's husband, however, doesn't _____ Americans, and seems to think they are perfectly _____. Joe sometimes doesn't _____ in front of Americans, hoping they won't know what he is. In the second scene, he goes further and actually _____ to be English.

JOE TAYLOR *and* JOANNE SMITH *sit at a table; pastry and tea in front of them;* JOANNE *has a small shoebox beside her.*

JOANNE: No, I didn't mean that! I love Stratford. I really do. And the Royal Shakespeare Company, it's –. It's world famous, isn't it? What more could you want? (*Beat.*) It's just –

5

JOE: Joanne, I know what you're going to say.

JOANNE: I don't think you can –

JOE: You're going to say, the problem with Stratford is –. Well to be brutally blunt, it's all the Americans. Right?

JOANNE: How did you –?   10

JOE: Look, I feel the same way. Every time I go there it drives me crazy.

JOANNE: You too? Professor Taylor, I can't tell you how –

JOE: I don't know what it is about the place. Attracts them like flies.

JOANNE: London's not nearly so bad.   15

JOE: They at least hesitate in London.

JOANNE: By and large they do.

JOE: But in Stratford! Last year I think six different people came up to me. I hadn't said anything. I had even avoided eye contact. But if they sniff you out as an American –   20

JOANNE: Which in Stratford does not take a bloodhound.

JOE: I tried once wearing a nice tweed cap. I loved this cap. Some guy from Louisiana nearly knocks me down, he was so excited to tell me he'd bought the same sort of cap in Edinburgh.*

JOANNE: I know they come right at you.   25

JOE: Why do I care where they're from, this is what I don't understand. So they happen to be American and so am I. So big deal.

JOANNE: Right.

JOE: We have nothing in common. I don't know –. They make the   30
whole thing feel cheap.

JOANNE: By 'the whole thing' you mean being here.

JOE: Absolutely.

JOANNE: I get that same feeling.

JOE: For you it must be –. Because you're actually living here.   35
You're a resident and everything. (*Beat*). Then to be taken for a tourist.

JOANNE: It drives me crazy. So I hardly go to Stratford any more. And never. Never in the summer.

JOE: *That* must be a nightmare. The summer.   40

JOANNE: Imagine your worst nightmare and then double it.

(*Pause. They sip their tea.*)

JOE: (*Takes a bite of a pastry.*) Delicious. Would you like to try –? (*She shakes her head.*)

JOANNE: I used to feel a little funny about it. They are after all from   45
my country. But –. (*Beat.*) Then you hear them shout.

JOE: (*Eating*) If they just acted like they were guests.

JOANNE: My husband doesn't mind. He finds them sort of –

---

* JOE *pronounces the* gh *as a strong g.*

JOE: But he's not American. So he's not the one being
50   embarrassed.

JOANNE: That's true. Well put. (*Beat.*) I'll explain it that way to him.
(*Short pause.*)
Sometimes when I'm in a shop I try not to say anything. I just
point. Maybe they'll think I'm English or something. Maybe that
55   I don't even speak English. That I'm foreign. So I point.

JOE: The accents some people have.

JOANNE: They don't hear themselves. (*Beat.*) Sometimes it's funny,
but sometimes –
(*Short pause.*)
60   Anyway.

JOE: Right. Anyway.
(*She starts to open the box.*)

JOANNE: It's good to talk to someone who –. Well –. You know.

JOE: I know. (*Offering her the last bite of pastry*) Are you sure?

65   JOANNE: No, thanks.
(*She starts to take out piles of tickets with rubber bands around
them.*)

JOE: (*Eating the last bite*) Incredible, the calibre of food sold in a
theatre.

70   JOANNE: Here's the last lot.

JOE: (*Eating*) Everyone – by the way – has been raving about the
seats we've had.

JOANNE: Good, I'm pleased to hear that. You never really know
what you'll get.

75   JOE: I don't think we've had one bad seat.

JOANNE: Knock wood. So – here's for this afternoon, the Lyttelton.
It's wonderful by the way. You'll have a great time.

JOE: Terrific.

JOANNE: (*Handing over bunches of tickets*) The Simon Gray is
80   tonight. (*Beat.*) It's short. (*Beat.*) Tomorrow's Stratford. Friday's
Stratford again. Then the day off. That's correct, isn't it?

JOE: (*Going over his list that he has taken out*) That's correct.

JOANNE: Good. (*Beat.*) Then there's Saturday night back at the
Barbican. I finally got *Les Mis*, on Monday.

85   JOE: Thank you. Mary and I saw it in New York. The kids'll love it.

JOANNE: Tuesday, the Royal Court.

JOE: What's there?

JOANNE: I forget. It's in previews.

JOE: Oh really. That could be fun.

90   JOANNE: Something very Royal Courtish to be sure.

JOE: I know what you mean.
   (*He laughs to himself.*)
JOANNE: Something at Wyndham's on Wednesday afternoon, then
   a free evening and you're gone on Thursday. So there you have
   the rest of it. (*Pushing the tickets toward him*) James, I'm afraid,   95
   is working late these days in the City. He sends his regrets about
   Wednesday night.
JOE: (*Looking at the tickets*) I'm sorry to hear –
JOANNE: But if you wouldn't mind my coming alone . . .
JOE: (*Looks up.*) Alone? Of course not! Why would we mind?   100
   (*Beat.*) James must be doing very well.
JOANNE: He is. He is. (*Beat.*) We're going to buy a boat.
   (*Beat.*)
JOE: We haven't decided on the restaurant. But I'll –
JOANNE: There's no rush. I'm home most nights. (*Beat.*) And there's   105
   a machine.
JOE: I'll call. When we've decided.

JOE TAYLOR *and an* AMERICAN MAN, *during the interval of the matinée.*
   JOE *has a rolled-up poster under his arm and eats ice-cream*
   from a cup; the AMERICAN *smokes a cigarette and looks through*   110
   a programme.

AMERICAN: They don't have any pictures of the actors in their
   costumes. (*Beat.*) Did you notice?
   (JOE *shakes his head.*)
   A shame. The costumes are terrific.   115
JOE: Please. (*Beat.*) Please, don't shout.
AMERICAN: He's good. (*Points to a picture.*) Don't you think he's
   good?
   (JOE *eats and nods.*)
   What a costume he's got. (*Beat.*) You got a poster. I was   120
   thinking of getting one. Which one did you get?
   (JOE *hesitates, then shows him.*)
   Maybe I'll get that one too.
JOE: There are plenty of other –
AMERICAN: Look here. (*Shows him an advertisement in the*   125
   programme.) They seem to have all kinds of shit. (*Reads:*) 'RSC
   Merchandise'. (*Beat.*) Posters. T-shirts. Records. Here's an RSC
   shopping bag. RSC address book. The Game of Shakespeare.
   What do you think that's about?
   (JOE *shrugs, looks away.*)   130

Maybe my niece would like that, she loves Monopoly. She kills
me at it. (*Laughs.*) She's ruthless. I wonder what kind of skills this
game teaches. (*Beat.*) So what part of the States do you come
from?

135   JOE: I'm British. I'm a naturalized British citizen. (*Beat.*) I tutor at
Oxford.
AMERICAN: No kidding. I'm in insurance.

Richard Nelson,
Some Americans Abroad

ACTIVITIES – STAGE **2**:

1 To check your understanding of these scenes quickly, say as briefly
as possible who, what or where (what place) is referred to in these
words:

the place (line 14)

here (lines 32 and 35)

they (in *they'll*, line 54)

Mary (line 85

the kids (in *the kids'll love it*, line 85)

James (line 95)

a machine (line 106)

he (in *he's good*, line 117)

they (line 126)

2 We said earlier in this section that, in a play, we sometimes have to
look beneath the surface of the words and guess what the
characters are thinking and feeling. Look at these lines and put
into your own, simple words what you think the person is really
saying:

JOE (line 16): They at least hesitate in London.

JOE (line 36): You're a resident and everything.

JOANNE (line 63): It's good to talk to someone who –. Well –. You
know.

JOE (line 101): James must be doing very well.

AMERICAN (line 112): They don't have any pictures of the actors in their costumes. Did you notice?

AMERICAN (line 132): I wonder what kind of skills this game teaches.

3 Although Joe and Joanne are so critical of the other Americans, the playwright reveals some characteristics of theirs which other countries think are typically American.

    (a) Look at lines 76–95, in which Joanne describes her programme for the students. What characteristic does this suggest?

    (b) Look at the references to her husband, in lines (95–102). Do you see anything American here?

    (c) Can you find other examples in the text?

ACTIVITIES – STAGE **3**:

1 One of the best ways to improve pronunciation and intonation is to read aloud dialogue from good, recent plays. Start by checking through the text silently. If there is any word you are not sure how to pronounce, ask your teacher. The teacher will then write up the words, marking the stress on them, like this:

    ☐☐   ☐   ☐

    Louisiana   incredible   calibre

2 Remember, as you read, to leave out stage directions like *They sip their tea*, but to pause for an instruction like *Pause* or *Beat*.

3 The teacher will divide the class into threes to read the parts of Joe, Joanne and the American. Don't insist that men read the men's parts or women the woman's, but do try to give them the right kind of voice and accent (especially the American in the second scene).

    As you read, your teacher will go around the class, listening.

4 The teacher will now choose three students to read the dialogue to the class.

ACTIVITIES – STAGE 4:

1 We are now going to write a short dialogue, using some of what we have learned in this chapter. Remember, as you work, some of these things about dialogue:

- – people do not say exactly what they mean. They give hints and suggestions
- – people interrupt themselves (line 8) and others (line 6)
- – they sometimes leave out important words (line 35)
- – they don't speak smoothly, without pause, but stop and start again. Put into your dialogue the instructions *Beat* and *Pause* to show where people are embarrassed or uncertain.

2 Here are some possible subjects for your dialogue. Your teacher will ask you to suggest others.

(a) Two people begin a conversation in a train in a foreign country. Because they both speak English, they don't realize for some time that they are from the same country.

(b) Someone starting a job in a new company speaks to an older employee. The older person doesn't know what country the new person comes from, and makes jokes about that country.

(c) Two people speaking English in a train think that the person opposite doesn't understand the language, and talk about him. He gets up to leave and says in perfect English, 'Goodbye. I've enjoyed your conversation.'

SIX: EXPLORING OTHER CULTURES

ACTIVITIES – STAGE 1:

1 A *culture* is a system of thoughts and beliefs that links together a group of people. (The word has other meanings – your teacher may want to tell you about them, to ask you to look them up in your dictionary.) These groups of people, for which we also use words like *community* and *society*, are often linked by:

History
Religion
Language
Skin colour or other physical similarities
Tradition and customs
Eating habits
Ways of dressing

First, to be sure you understand this important word, think of a *culture* everyone in the class knows. Your teacher will write up some examples.

2 Think of a similar word to *culture* in your language. But beware of making an exact translation – few words translate directly from one language to another. Beware also of the word *race*. It is used rarely, and very carefully, in present-day English. Please discuss why this is so.

3 Look at the list in Activity 1. How many of these words and phrases apply to the examples of cultures you thought of in that exercise?

4 You probably think of your country as one culture, but today most countries of the world contain many cultures. These may add to and enrich the country. Sadly, they also divide many countries of the world, and are the reason for some of the worse persecutions and wars. So it is important for you to be able to express clearly in English your own beliefs and opinions on the subject.

5 Look at the following list. How many of them are cultures? Put a
  ring around those.

  – the German-speaking Swiss

  – the Japanese

  – Turkish guest-workers in Germany

  – Vietnamese refugees in California

  – an international school in New York

  – Tamils in Sri Lanka

  – Irish, French, Chinese and American Catholics

  – girls who wear jeans

  – a football team

  – an orchestra

6 Do you, yourself, feel part of any culture that is separate from the
  main culture of your country? Does this cause you any problems?

ACTIVITIES – STAGE 2:

1 Now we are going to read part of an article by Meera Syall. She is
  an actress and writer. Her parents came to England from New
  Delhi in 1960. She was born and grew up in England, and has a
  degree in English and drama from a British university. She is
  married to a British-born fellow Indian, and has one small
  daughter. She wrote the screenplay for the film *Bhaji on the Beach*,
  and writes for the British newspaper the *Guardian*. British readers
  find what she writes funny and revealing not only about her own
  culture, but about British culture.

  (a) Looking back at the list in Activity 1 (on page 95) – history,
      language etc. – how many of these cultural differences do you
      think would apply to Meera Syall and her family?
  (b) As you read, note whether any of these differences is actually
      mentioned in the article.
  (c) What do your findings, in (b) above, tell you about Meera
      Syall herself, and the people she is writing about?

2 The main subject of Meera Syall's article is marriage, and how it works in her culture. As you read, look for two eight-letter words beginning with the letter A which describe kinds of marriage. Write these below.

A _____ marriage   A _____ marriage

Which of these does Meera Syall say is the way it is actually done in the Asian community?

3 Why does Meera use the word *Western* to contrast with *Asian*?

It's a sticky one, this whole area of how we are represented. The awkward thing about clichés is that they do contain germs of truth; black musicians do outclass and dominate the music scene, some arranged marriages do end in unhappiness and sometimes violence. But once the clichés appear in the papers, they become   5
the whole truth and nothing but because only those of us who live in those communities know the larger picture. Therefore, the only coverage I've ever seen about marriage in the Asian community has focused on when the system has gone wrong.

Take my cousin Shaila, the only Asian girl I knew when I was   10
growing up who downed lagers, wore Doc Martens and once told a room full of aunties that every thinking person should swing both ways. Boyfriends, she had 'em panting after her, all shades and sizes, she reaches twenty-nine and what does she do? Announces to my uncle and auntie she'd quite like to meet a few Asian guys   15
with a view to settling down and could they set up a few tea parties please? No one imagines that free-thinking Asian women born and brought up here choose to enter this system. What they do imagine is a brute of a father, usually a religious maniac with a fetish for floggings, dragging some helpless fourteen-year-old out   20
of school straight to the altar, the bridegroom being a distant cousin who's a yak breeder with a hare lip, needing a British passport etc, etc . . .

In fact, arranged marriage is in some circles now called assisted marriage, because of the openness with which parents   25
and children consult each other on marital matters. This is how it now happens round my way; young Sanjay or Shaila tell their folks they're about ready to consider settling down; mother says, 'Oh there's that lovely X, so and so's son/daughter doing accountancy, drives a Saab . . .' Sanjay/Shaila tells Mother X is a   30

prize dork and they wouldn't piss on X if X was on fire, so they
continue debating the pros and cons of the children of their
parents' friends until they find one that doesn't make the other faint
with horror. Mother phones up Y's mother, the 'youngsters' as
35   they're known are left to meet up at their own discretion and report
back. If they survive a couple of dates without throwing up or
dying of boredom, if in fact they even find they like each other,
then the parents get involved, a more formal pow-wow of the two
tribes is arranged and maybe, maybe, an engagement will be
40   announced. BUT at any time, the children are free to say no and
walk away, that's the bottom line. There. Not so bad, is it?

What most Westerners, and to be fair, some Asians, find hard
to reconcile is the premeditated nature of this arrangement. There
are no illusions as to why you're meeting X or Y at the pictures,
45   your eyes have not met across a crowded room; indeed, you know
your looks, weight, earning capacity and family cleanliness have
been thoroughly discussed before you even get to the first-date
stage. You are meeting with a view to marriage, and what's more,
you ain't got the next year or so to think it over. Generally, a
50   decision is expected within a few months; after all, the serious
social vetting has already been done, no danger of hidden
skeletons or a shady background; your mother's cousin knew his
auntie's nephew back home and that's virtually a written
guarantee. All the questions a Western couple ask over months of
55   'going out' are already answered, you know you have similar
long-term goals, attitudes to kids; the rest is up to you.

'But it's so . . . business like! Where's the romance?' I hear Mrs
A. from Surrey asking me. Well, my auntie Usha would reply, 'You
think romance is a basis for marriage? Look at your divorce rate!
60   You English want the thrills you feel at the beginning to last all the
time, so when you get bored, you move on to the next partner, and
the next . . . We know lasting love grows slowly, out of give and
take. Our thrills come later . . .'

Meera Syall

ACTIVITIES – STAGE 3:

1   Now read the text again, more slowly, and as you do, list under the
two headings below the stages a couple go through as they get
married: how they meet, when they fall in love, when their
families meet, and so on.

For the heading WESTERN MARRIAGE you get only hints in the text: you must draw on your own knowledge, and, if you are not from a Western country, you must draw on books, films, and television. In listing the steps, use present tenses as Meera Syall does (*Mother phones up Y's mother,* etc).

WESTERN MARRIAGE   ASIAN MARRIAGE

When someone says
I LOVE YOU!
RUN for YOUR LIFE!

ACTIVITIES – STAGE 4:

1 When we read a text like this, we are looking for insights rather than facts. We are seeking understanding of something new to us. So we are not thinking in terms of true or false but whether things

are *probable* or *improbable*. Reading the article again, decide which
of the following statements is probable, which improbable.

PROBABLE   IMPROBABLE

(a) The British and other
    Western nations have a
    clear understanding of so-
    called arranged marriage.

(b) All arranged marriages are
    happy.

(c) All arranged marriages are
    unhappy.

(d) Meera Syall's cousin Shaila
    was unattractive to look at.

(e) Lager was served at her
    wedding.

(f) There is usually a very
    wide difference in age
    between Asian men and
    the women they marry.

(g) Asian parents prefer a
    husband with a good job
    and a secure income.

(h) The first meeting of an
    Asian couple is full of
    surprises.

2 Match the person with the description.

Cousin Shaila	She is an imaginary person Meera Syall
A brute of a father	uses to represent a typical English woman.
Sanjay	He is an imaginary Asian man who has
Mrs A. from Surrey	reached the stage where he wants to get married.
Auntie Usha	
	She wore trendy English clothes and had opinions that shocked other Asian women.
	He is the person most Westerners think really arranges Asian marriages.
	She thinks Westerners should question their own marriage customs.

ACTIVITIES – STAGE 5:

1 Look at these expressions of opinion on the subject of marriage. First, tick (✓) those with which you think Meera Syall would agree.

   (a) Marriage should be based on true love, probably at first sight, and nothing else.

   (b) Before entering into marriage, couples ought to know a lot about each other.

   (c) They should also know something about the other person's family, background and culture.

   (d) Couples must be free to choose each other, without interference from families.

   (e) Parents should play the major part in choosing marriage partners for their children.

   (f) Husbands ought to choose wives, rather than wives husbands.

2 These statements contain three of the structures most commonly used to express opinions in English. One of these is *must* in statement (d). Find and underline the other two.

3 Now the teacher will divide the class into several groups, to discuss your opinions on marriage. Include in your discussion the ways in which marriage is changing, in your own and other countries. Draw on your own experience of marriages which were happy, unhappy, or simply working relationships which lasted. Try as far as you can to agree within your groups. Then choose a reporter, who will tell the class what you felt, using the three grammatical structures for expressing opinion you found in Activity 2.

SEVEN: EXPLORING NATIONAL ATTITUDES

ACTIVITIES – STAGE 1:

1 Which do you think tells us more about a country:

- – its attitudes to war, peace and politics;
- – its attitudes to everyday subjects like children, old people, clothes and food?

2 Look at the three subjects below, and try to say, simply, what you think the people of your country feel about them. Then think of another country you know something about, which has opposite attitudes to these three:

- – medical matters - doctors, hospitals, medicines;
- – hygiene - worry about keeping people, houses, etc. very clean;
- – babies.

3 You are going to read now part of an article written by Vicki Woods, an English writer, for a British magazine, *The Spectator*. She gives you all the other information you need to know to enjoy her article, and the few words you don't know you should be able to guess.

4 As you read the first part of the article, try to match the person with the correct description of that person's attitude to the baby.

PERSON	ATTITUDE
Vicki Woods	Generous, enthusiastic, with warm feelings and the words to express them
Her daughter	
Her 14-year old son	Highly nervous about hygiene
Jeffrey Junior's mother	Fairly interested, wanting to touch
	Uninterested and superior

Hands Off My Baby!

I went to visit an American baby in New York: his mother is a friend of mine and lives in the meat-packing district, which is a lot smarter than it sounds. The baby's father, a banker, is called Jeffrey; so the baby is called Jeffrey Junior and is known to his

5 family as J.J. He is their first child, long-awaited and much-loved, and his entry into the world, at a fashionable New York hospital, was very expensive. I visited him, with my children, when he was three months old, and was delighted to find him tactfully wearing my gift of a little apple-green, Italian outfit printed with big red

10 ladybirds. My daughter chose it at Harrods; it took all morning. He looked a treat, little J.J. His mother woke him up for us. I put my arms out and started tuning up the lengthy raga with which women welcome boy-babies to the world (girl-babies are just as welcome, obviously, but with different adjectives). Thus: 'O Jeffrey Junior,

15 you *handsome* boy, just *look* at you, so big and *strong*, how *intelligent*-looking, how *alert*, come here, you angelic thing, you, give him to me at *once* –' but his mother held him tight. 'One second!' she said, speaking very fast. 'I *know* you're British, I *know* you're going to get me for this, but I *have* to say it! I *have* to

20 ask!' Ask what? 'It isn't me – it's the *doctor*, believe me. My paediatrician *insisted*; he said I have to tell everybody to – everybody that holds the baby to – picks up the baby to –' To what, in heaven's name? 'To wash their hands first.'

I looked at my hands and blushed with embarrassment and so

25 did she, but she ploughed on gamely, righteously. 'Omigod, look at your face, you think I'm nuts!' 'Erm, you are nuts,' I said. 'Please! Bear with me! I know you're from England and you think

I'm crazy! It's to cut down the risk of cross-infection! My paed
insists! Even my mother! The bathroom is right here – soap and
towels are ready. Please! Don't look at me like that!'   30

Well, I tidied away the look on my face and went into the little
cloakroom to scrub up. I felt completely ridiculous and oddly filthy.
'Mine are clean,' said my daughter, reaching out a finger to poke
the baby, but I hauled her towards the wash-basin, too, before
there was another cross-cultural outburst. My 14-year-old son   35
folded his grimy hands over his chest. Not touching it, OK?

Vicki Woods,
The Spectator

ACTIVITIES – STAGE 2:

1 Read the text again, and, as you do, judge which of these
statements you think are *likely* to be true. As in the last chapter, we
are not talking about facts, but about judgments we make, as we
read, about what is likely or unlikely.

LIKELY   UNLIKELY

(Put a ✓ under
your answer.)

(a) Having a baby in America can be very
expensive.

(b) Americans do not greatly value children.

(c) Vicki Woods visited her friend with the
new baby out of a sense of duty, because
she thought she should.

(d) The British are more conscious of hygiene
and health than the Americans.

(e) The American baby's mother was embarrassed, but determined to do what the
doctor had told her.

(f) Vicki Woods was very angry when told
she had to wash her hands.

2 Now we are going to read a later part of the same article, in which
Vicki Woods goes to a different country. What do you think will
happen there? What different national attitudes do you think she
will discover?

3 The country is Italy. Do you want to change the predictions you made in the last question?

4 Now read this section, and decide how well you guessed what you would find in it.

After I'd had a beautiful daughter, we took them both to Italy: the daughter in arms and the son kicking about in his new Start-Rites and a Paddington Bear sun-hat. My daughter was a green-eyed blonde, and at six months old a fat cartoon of a baby. I couldn't
5   keep hold of her. It wasn't just a question of being poked, stroked or tickled – she was lifted bodily out of my arms every single time we went out. Italian mammas took her. They shrieked with delight and passed her from hand to hand among their families. *'O che bella bionda bimba! Che bellissimi occhi!'* they said, while they
10   kissed her fat little feet and poked her hamster cheeks with unwashed fingers and curled her wispy ringlets over their brilliant manicures. I waited rather helplessly to get her back each time: there was no hurrying this adoration. My daughter simpered and cooed at the worshippers. *'Grazie tanto,'* they said politely,
15   handing her over. I began to like Italy a lot. We stood outside the Duomo in Siena, realising that we were hampered in our desire to see inside it by having two children under two with us. I said, 'Oh, well, next time.'
        Sitting in a slice of shade to one side of the entrance was a line
20   of old women dressed in black: they watched us turn away from the cathedral door, carrying the children. *'Signora!'* shouted one of them, patting her knee and holding out her arms. My husband said, 'We can't just leave the children with them.' And I said, 'Of course we can.' I had the hang of a nation that liked children by
25   now. The senior crone took the *bellissima bionda bimba* and three others swooped down on the boy, who opened his mouth to yell with fear until one of them popped into it something unhygienic and sugary that she just happened to have on her. The senior crone took me by the wrist, drew a half circle on my watch face to
30   show me how long they'd baby-sit and waved us into the cathedral. When we came out after half an hour, they handed the children back, *Grazie tanto.*

Vicki Woods,
The Spectator

ACTIVITIES – STAGE **3**:

1 Discuss, first with a partner and then with the class, how well you guessed what you would find in this part of the text. Which student in the class guessed most correctly?

2 This text has many good examples of the way in which, as you read, you guess the meaning of unfamiliar words partly by the context, and partly by your common sense and knowledge of the world – what babies, small girls, fourteen-year-old boys, new mothers, older women are actually like. Working in this way, choose what you think is the meaning of the word from the pair of choices.

tactfully	(a) Politely, showing good manners
	(b) Impolitely, showing bad manners
tuning up	(a) Getting ready to perform
	(b) Singing correctly
raga	(a) A piece of piano music
	(b) A kind of song
paediatrician	(a) A nurse
	(b) A doctor specializing in babies
blushed	(a) Turned pink or red
	(b) Turned pale or white
filthy	(a) Very clean
	(b) Very dirty
grimy	(a) Very clean
	(b) Very dirty
poked	(a) Kissed
	(b) Touched with one finger
stroked	(a) Rubbed gently with one hand
	(b) Hit hard
tickled	(a) Touched in a way to make you laugh
	(b) Cried
shrieked	(a) Made a high noise of pleasure
	(b) Whispered quietly
hampered	(a) Prevented someone from doing something
	(b) Hesitated
crone	(a) An old woman
	(b) A bird

3 Look at the first part of the text again, at lines 14–17, beginning 'Oh Jeffrey Junior . . .' Vicki Woods says she would say something similar to a girl baby, with different adjectives. Try to say what some of these adjectives might be.

4 Do you have in your language a special way of talking to babies, called in English 'baby talk'? What do you do to the words when you use 'baby talk'? Do you ever use it in other situations apart from talking to babies?

ACTIVITIES – STAGE **4**:

1 Now that you have read and worked with the text, look back at the first question in this chapter, about national attitudes. Working in pairs, choose two subjects, one an everyday subject like babies, the other a more serious subject like death or religion. Contrast your country's attitudes on these with those of some other country you know.

2 To report to the class, look back at some of the ways we have described attitudes in this chapter.
   Here are some adjectives we have used, with the prepositions that normally follow them:

   generous to   *interested/uninterested in*
   enthusiastic about   *nervous about/over*

Here are some further phrases we often use in describing attitudes. Notice carefully the prepositions that follow them.

   opposed to   *disapproving of*
   believing in   *keen on*
   in favour of   *indifferent to*

Use some of these expressions in reporting, taking care to follow them with correct prepositions.

3 When you have reported, please write a short paragraph in which you contrast the attitudes of the two countries to the two subjects. Try to include a little story to illustrate at least one of the attitudes. Use some of the expressions in Activity 2 and some words you know for contrast, like *but, however,* and so on.

4 Vicki Woods says (line 4) her daughter was a 'fat cartoon of a baby'. Draw a fat cartoon of a baby. Your teacher will put them up, and the class will choose which is the best.

EIGHT: COMPARING NATIONAL ATTITUDES

ACTIVITIES – STAGE 1:

1 In Chapter Seven, we looked at one person's experience of national attitudes. Now we are going to compare the ways in which two countries look at one another. Here are some of the ways in which one country forms its attitudes towards another. If you can think of other ways, add them to the list:

- reading about other countries in the newspapers of our own country
- reading other countries' newspapers
- reading books
- watching films and television
- meeting people from another country in our own
- visiting the country as tourists
- visiting the country as travellers (if in doubt about these two, look back at Chapter Four in this Unit)
- living and working in another country.

2 Rank these ways (including any you have added) into the order in which you think they are reliable ways of forming attitudes. Put the most reliable first.

ACTIVITIES – STAGE **2**:

1 Now you are going to read parts of a book by Beppe Severgnini, who, as an Italian journalist for the newspaper *Il Giornale*, worked in England from 1984–88. His book, *Inglese,* was a great success in Italy, and was published in England in 1991, translated by Paula Pugsley.

First, read all three parts very quickly, answering only this one question: which sentence ending, *a, b,* or *c,* best sums up the text?

Beppe Severgnini's overall view of the English is:
(a) sharp and cruel.
(b) friendly but critical
(c) one of reverence and deep respect.

2 Then read the three parts again, and, for each of the ideas below, choose whether the idea occurs in Part One, Two or Three. If it does not occur in any of the parts, put 0.

IDEA	PART
England is now a less law-abiding country than in the recent past.	
The idea we met in the Pont cartoon and the Keith Waterhouse text – that the British prefer the past to the present – is confirmed.	
British lower-class people have a dislike of foreigners, based upon their knowledge of foreign products like beer and hi-fi systems.	
British working-class people envy the rich, and like mixing with them.	
Peregrine Worsthorne, a political opponent of Mrs Thatcher, thought that she had made the British too controlled and like socialists.	
Margaret Thatcher saw Britain as an independent country with its own nuclear weapons.	

The bravery and commitment which once made the
English good soldiers, now makes them football hooligans.

British class tastes and habits are well-established, and
seem unlikely to change.

Part One

The class system survives because everyone seems happy with his
lot. The upper classes take pride in their genuine or pretended
eccentricities, the middle classes delight in looking at their well
mown lawns, and the lower classes sit happily in front of the box
5   watching darts, or staring at the big bosoms on page three. They
don't want change. The Italian worker sees a beautiful car and
says, 'I'd love to have it', the British worker dismisses it: 'Rich man's
stuff'. The average Italian is delighted to be asked to an important
wedding: afterwards he will talk for weeks on end about it. His
10   British counterpart hates every minute of it and longs to be back
where he belongs, with his friends at the pub. In Italy people are
apprehensive but they are always on the go, restless and busy; in
Great Britain they are quiet and contented: they like things to be as
they have always been.
15   There is no doubt that the British are obsessed with their past: a
new museum opens every week. It is a world record but not
something to be really proud of: while the rest of the world
manufacture goods, they produce tradition. Many have protested
against this tendency to turn Great Britain into one huge museum
20   but to no avail. Margaret Thatcher herself met with opposition
every time she wanted to introduce anything new. It happened
with the pound coin replacing the note, with the new yellow
telephone boxes instead of the traditional red ones, and with the
new maroon European passport taking the place of the old stiff
25   blue British one with its little window.

Part Two

The tabloids and television bear the responsibility for yet another
characteristic of the lower class, an extraordinary lack of interest in
what happens on the other side of the Channel. It is not
30   xenophobia, because that would require some knowledge of the
people you despise. The working class simply ignores foreigners.
They are prepared to take an interest in them only when they
produce cheaper hi-fi systems (Japanese), or drink more beer

(Germans), or lose a war (Argentinians), or when you can insult
them: when the *Sun* talks about the French it does not write   35
'French', it writes 'frogs'. Top of the list of dislikes is the European
Community, which is accused of being up to all sorts of dirty tricks.
Margaret Thatcher understood this very well. She was tough with
the EEC, while promising lasting political independence backed by
nuclear weapons. The British armies of old marched to her tune.   40

Part Three

The trouble with this courteous and educated nation comes when
courtesy and education are not there. The British are not the same
people when they are drunk, when they get angry, when they
become fanatical. In the old days those 'qualities' helped them to   45
win wars. Now drunkards, thugs and fanatics all go to football
stadia and we know full well what they are capable of. Socially,
these people belong to the middle and the lower classes. The
middle class itself is reaching new depths of depravity, with the
increase in child abuse cases and sex crimes. One almost regrets   50
the days when its favourite form of crime was poisoning. The
editor of the *Sunday Telegraph* the staunch Conservative, Sir
Peregrine Worsthorne, wrote not long ago that all this is Mrs
Thatcher's fault: she was the one who freed 'Homo Britannicus'
from many constraints, without thinking that he could make bad   55
use of his newly found freedom. Others have noted how surprised
and grateful pedestrians are when a car stops for them at zebra
crossings. This is new: until recently pedestrians crossed self-
confidently, their heads high: they knew they were exercising their
right. This is but a small symptom of a greater uneasiness: the   60
country is rougher, solidarity and compassion have gone out of
fashion, and people rightly or wrongly feel vulnerable.

Beppe Severgnini,
Inglese

3 Finally, try to sum up this journalist's attitudes to the past and the
present of the English, and guess what he feels about the
future. Think carefully about the tenses you use for each, and write
complete sentences.

THE PAST

THE PRESENT

THE FUTURE

ACTIVITIES – STAGE 3:

1 Now we are going to look at an opposite set of attitudes: what the English think of the Italians. You will read a story from the *Daily Telegraph*. As you read, choose the best way of ending each sentence below.

(a) The opinions of Italians in the story are those of...

Sonia Purnell.

an official paper from the British government.

a British businessman.

(b) The Italians in the Italian embassy in London who read it were...

frivolous.

angry.

frightened.

(c) The attitude towards the Italians was...

reassuring to businessmen.

based on stereotypes and unflattering.

based on years of careful research.

(d) The document, issued by the British, said that the British...

lacked good shopping facilities.

had a political system the Italians admired.

had too much bureaucracy.

Official advice on selling to the Italians

They are loud, late and don't tell the truth

Italians are frivolous, loud, late and they don't tell the truth – according to a Government guide for exporters. The official guide also urges businessmen to refrain from making jokes about the Mafia.

5   Not surprisingly, perhaps, this assessment has not gone down too well with the Italians themselves.

The Italian Embassy in London reacted angrily and not at all frivolously, to a Department of Trade and Industry paper called *Contacts with the Italian Business Community*.

10   An embassy spokesman said yesterday: 'We don't want to

comment publicly, but we do hold very strong private views about it.'

The seven-page document gives several warnings that Italians regularly fail to tell the truth or keep their word.

They are 'prone to telling foreign business contacts what they think the contact wants to hear rather than what they themselves really think'.

It also says: 'Don't expect your Italian counterparts to make a formal recording of verbal agreements reached, or to adhere to them too strictly.'

The DTI also instructs exporters not to 'assume your host will undertake the follow-up action he/she promised'.

And it gives tips on the social behaviour of Italian business people, describing them as 'noisy, often exuberant'. It advises: 'Body language is important; try using your hands as you speak to emphasise points you are making – ie don't be stuffy.'

Italians are also said to be hopeless at timekeeping, and the DTI advises patience to Britons who are forced to hang around waiting for appointments.

The paper explains: 'Occasionally your host may not even be in the office at the hour he/she agreed to see you, don't get annoyed! Don't lose your temper – by doing so you will merely lose face.'

When Italians eventually do turn up, it would be unwise, says the DTI, to expect them to be well-prepared for the meeting.

'The theme of Italian life is spontaneity!' say the men from the ministry.

Italians are also said to be evasive about their comprehension of English. 'Even those who speak English may not understand as much as you think they do, and will be unwilling to court ridicule by revealing this.'

But they certainly like to hold court. 'Some Italians are poor listeners; they will want to do a lot of the talking. Be patient!'

The guide also spells out what flowers to give Italians. 'Never send chrysanthemums (they are reserved for funerals), and roses are better avoided because of their romantic connotations.'

One successful British exporter, who is half-Italian, said he was 'ashamed at the guide's simplistic racist stereotypes', adding that it could harm the reputation of the British abroad.

But the DTI is reassuring in what it claims is the foreigner's view of Britain. It says Italians envy the UK 'for its relatively straightforward political system and lack of bureaucracy . . . and good shopping facilities'.

Sonia Purnell,
The Daily Telegraph
8 December 1993

ACTIVITIES – STAGE 4:

1 Read the text again. In it, you find many different attitudes towards Italians. With a partner, choose the *three* of these that interest you most. Use your own words, as far as you can, in reporting to the class what these attitudes are.

Use the grammar for **reported speech** in your answers (your teacher may want to remind you of this).

The British government document *said* that the Italians *were* loud, late and *didn't* tell the truth.

Notice how the grammar requires different, past tenses after the verb *said*, rather than present tenses like those in the first sentence of the story.

To help you to vary your sentences, here are some possible beginnings, and some possible verbs to replace *said*.

Beginnings	**Verbs**
The Government guide	*stated*
The Department of Trade and Industry paper	*claimed*
	warned
The British officials	*explained*

2 In these texts about attitudes, we have met some nouns ending in *-y*, like *spontaneity*, and some adjectives from which they come,

loquacity

TACITURNITY

like *frivolous*. We use many of these frequently when describing our attitudes both to people individually, and to countries (and cultures).

3 Here is a list of such nouns. Some of them are difficult words, but they are all items that advanced students should know. Working from the noun, please fill in the adjective from which it comes, and then say as simply as you can what the *adjective* means. You may find a synonym, but not all English words have an exact synonym. Work in groups of four. Between you, you should be able to get most of the answers. If you cannot, use an English/English dictionary.

NOUN	ADJECTIVE	MEANING
loquacity	loquacious	talkative
frivolity		
taciturnity		
spontaneity		
dishonesty		
hypocrisy		
mendacity		
insincerity		
bravery		
unreliability		
punctuality		
vivacity		
eccentricity		
ingenuity		
creativity		
stupidity		
indomitability		
impassivity		

4 To help us remember the meaning of these words, we will try to get across their meaning by **mime** – acting out the meaning silently.

Working in pairs now, choose a word you would like to mime.
Write it down, then show it silently to the teacher, who will
check it off so that no nouns are repeated. You will have a few
minutes to work out your mime. Then come in front of the class
to do your mime. The other students will try to guess your word.

5 To finish this section (and while you are in a mood to act), prepare
with the same partner a short scene, including words, in which an
Italian (as seen by the British government) meets a working-class
Englishman (as seen by Beppe Severgnini). No violence, please.

NINE: CHANGING NATIONALITY

ACTIVITIES – STAGE 1:

1 The subject of this chapter is people changing their nationality. Both authors of this book know about it. Mel's parents came to England from the continent of Europe, Ben from America. You, perhaps, have some experience, too, which you will have a chance to discuss later. First, look at this text about changing nationality. Find words from the group below to fill in the gaps.

When you arrive in a new country, hoping to live there, you are officially an _____, and you will also be described as an _____, which is another way of saying foreigner. In the eyes of your own countrymen, you are an _____, because you choose to live in a different country. In your adopted country, you will certainly be made to feel like an _____, especially when you first encounter the _____ who ask you a lot of questions, using their own language, which is called both _____ and _____. They will make you _____ in many _____, ask to see your own official _____, including _____ from people who know you to say you are of good character, and sworn statements, or _____. If you are lucky, they will give you a _____ to stay for a short time, and you may hope eventually to be _____, or made a _____ of that country. You will probably never really feel like a _____, but when you have lived there a long time, you will at least become _____, and feel less foreign. Then you can proudly show your own _____, and, you hope, have nothing more to do with _____ or _____, two words for the same thing – and a thing the world we live in has too much of!

bureaucracy	forms	expatriate
jargon	fill	affidavits
alien	officialdom	permit
passport	citizen	authorities
naturalized	assimilated	testimonials
immigrant	documents	officialese
native	outsider	

2 You will find some of these words in the texts we are going to read. More importantly, you will need them to discuss the texts and their subject. Your teacher will now, with your help, mark the stress on the words, like this:

☐

permit

You will then practise pronouncing the words in pairs. Notice that *permit* is one of those words that changes its stress to show you the difference between the noun and the verb with the same spelling. Can you think of one more example of such a word?

ACTIVITIES – STAGE **2**:

1 We are going to do something completely different with the two texts in this section. These activities are to help you to learn to read confidently and efficiently on your own, without a teacher.

First, number yourselves around the class: One, two, one, two, one, two etc. All the ones form a group at one end, all the twos at another. Choose one student to guide your work.

2 Each group will have its own text. Group One reads text One. Group Two reads text Two. But before you read, plan your activities.

3 Both texts come from *The New Yorker*. This is an American weekly magazine, published in New York but read all over the world. It is used by teachers in many American schools.

You know what the subject of this section is. Together, before you read, decide on one question which will enable you to get the general meaning of your text in one quick reading.

4 Read quickly, compare your answers.

5 Go through the text more slowly, working only on vocabulary you think is really important (using some of the methods of guessing we have done in this book). Concentrate on the story told in your text.

6 Now leave your groups, return to your seats, and divide into pairs
– each pair a one and a two. *Leave your texts and all papers behind.*
You are just to talk now, not read or write.

7 What do your two texts have in common? How are they different?
Tell each other the story of your text – not just the events, but
how you are made to feel about them.

Text One

Expatriate Games

I recently became an American citizen. Nothing unusual in that,
except that I am – was – British, and, as a rule, the British
expatriate is notoriously loyal to the home country. 'What on earth
did you do that for?' my mother wanted to know when I
telephoned her and reported the terrible news.   5

In order to become a citizen, I had to fill out many forms
and then, some months later, take a test on United States history
and government. The form part was easy: I asserted that I had
never been a member of the Waffen S.S., and I swore that I
had never had anything to do with Communists or the Soviet   10
Union, although this was not strictly true. I visited Russia on a
surreal trip from Oxford in March, 1975 – post-Bill Clinton. My
girlfriend was writing a thesis on Dostoyevski and the Russian
Orthodox Church. We had dinner in Leningrad with Boris
Pasternak's son. He asked me if I was Jewish. When I replied that I   15
was, he told me that many Russian Orthodox priests in the city
were in fact converted Jews. I didn't believe him. Later in the trip, a
boy in a floppy-eared fur hat standing guard over Dostoyevski's
snowy tomb (I think he was in the drug business) asked me to mail
him Pink Floyd albums.   20

I was nonchalant about the test part. I thought I could skip the
recommended books with impunity. I turned up at the J.F.K.
Building in downtown Boston for my interview at 8:30 A.M.,
imagining I would be alone, but the room was packed with early-
morning appointees. Some of us had to wait until midday for our   25
turn. Almost everybody was deeply engrossed in his or her primer.
I remained snobbishly unworried.

Interviews were conducted behind screens or in small rooms. In
some cases, it was possible to overhear what was going on. A

30   Chinese man who had been sitting behind me got a terrible going
      over. 'When's Pearl Harbor Day?' his interrogator repeated.
      'When is it? You don't understand what I'm saying, do you?' The
      man's wife was called into the room. I thought she would be asked
      to translate, but in fact she was curtly informed that her husband
35   had failed. Next was my Syrian neighbor: he disappeared for an
      hour. When he came out, I asked him about the questions. 'Search
      and Seizure,' he replied. 'The Bill of Rights.'
           'You're kidding!' I said.
           'And worse,' he added.
40   Now I started to panic. I borrowed a book from an old Russian
      man – nearly wrestled it from his hands – but the words swam in
      front of my eyes. I couldn't concentrate. Meanwhile, another
      person of color was being given the business: '*What* do we do on
      the Fourth of July? What do we celebrate? Do you know what I'm
45   saying? Do you know your own *name*?' By now, I was starting to
      rationalize. I didn't want to be American anyway. I'd have to do
      jury duty. Why be a citizen of a country that harasses its
      prospective immigrants?
           I was called in. First, I received an apology for having had to
50   wait. Second, another apology, because my questioner was sure
      she wasn't going to be as knowledgeable about American culture
      as I was. Third, an apology that I had to be asked questions at all.
      But here goes. Question 1: What are the three branches of
      government? 'Well,' I said, 'there's the judiciary and the legislature
55   . . .' 'And?' 'And the . . .' My questioner did everything she could
      with encouraging facial expressions to coax the answer out of me.
      Finally, I chirped brightly and hopefully 'The President?' 'The
      executive,' she corrected me, nodding her head. Question 2: Who
      is your district's congressional representative? 'Barney Frank.' End
60   of test.
           A couple of weeks later, I stopped in at a local coffee shop with
      my son and ran into my congressional representative. It was
      Sunday morning; he was in a jogging suit and looked ever so
      much as if he wanted to be left alone. But it was not to be. I had to
65   tell him my story. 'Yes,' he said, panting. 'We've had a lot of
      trouble with those I.N.S. people.' Barney tried to move toward the
      door. I stood in his way. Suddenly, I felt empowered. My
      impending citizenship was granting me the right to harass
      someone. It wasn't my accent that was pinning Barney to the wall
70   but my fresh and unimpeachable American credentials. My son
      tugged at my arm. 'Come on, Dad,' he said. But in the sunlit

doorway I continued to exercise my tyrannical democratic right, and I told poor Mr. Frank exactly the same story again.

Jonathan Wilson,
The New Yorker
5 July 1993

Text Two

Waiting In Room 3–120

As everyone in America knows, you can be a New Yorker without quite being an American. I've lived in this city for many years with a 'green card,' as a Permanent Resident Alien. The Immigration and Naturalization Service is calling in green cards as ancient as my own; an officer at J.F.K. gave me an appointment to visit the   5
I.N.S., downtown. The morning of the day he named, six or seven hundred people were patiently waiting at the front doors of the Javits Building, in Federal Plaza, and a couple of hundred others (with 'appointments') were lined up beside a shabby hedge to enter a door on the side. In front and in back of me, people   10
clutching instruction sheets like my own ('Go Directly to Third Floor Info Area, Room 3–120') shuffled forward by inches. The streets beyond the hedge were lined with photograph-and-notary joints and legal offices ('Green Cards,' *'Todos los Servicios,'* 'Translations $35 and Up'). Camp followers in grimy petticoats,   15
these establishments serve and depend on the bureaucracy; the same anxious, humble, never-ending crowd flows through them all, wearing tracks in the linoleum and rubbing corners off the desks.

A young Chinese woman rushed past us, waving a sheaf of photocopies. The baby strapped to her chest wore a look of   20
astonishment; his spiky tussock of blue-black hair wafted up and down. One by one, we went in – passing under the arch of the metal detector, with its sign informing us that our weapons would be confiscated and not returned. On the X-ray, the contents of my handbag looked unfamiliar, like a cache of bones. My identity   25
was leaching out as well. I had no depth, no past, no city; I was an applicant among a thousand such, trapped in eternal anterooms. When the elevator disgorged us – the woman in a sari; the dazed Old Country grandma leaning on a young man's arm; the Hispanic moppet in scarlet frills – Room 3–120 was felt as a   30
muffled roar. People milled in the doorway of the room – a long, narrow, modern chamber with a ceiling mean-spiritedly low. There

was a babel of languages. 'Keep moving! Through the *door!*' an
employee bellowed, making shooing motions.

35   Red numbers mounted at an excruciating, electronic crawl above
the counters of the immigration officers, safe behind a wall of
glass, and then flashed for a peremptory moment ('Number 738,
Window Eleven! Last call!'). Several hundred people stood about
with folded arms or leaned against the wall under makeshift,
40   crudely lettered signs. Several hundred others sat staring at the
numbers from rows of tomato-colored plastic chairs. Many had
arrived with family and friends: tribal huddles of jokesters and
seat-savers and designated English-speakers, who stood ready (if
need arose) to swim forward and press elucidatory lips to the
45   speaking-holes in the wall of glass. People stared at the fingerprint
charts on their laps as if some answer lay in the ashy whorls. The
woman handing out numbers only pursed her mouth if people
asked her things. 'No Information Questions,' said her sign. A
person's head could burst in the steamy air of Room 3–120; you
50   could *die* of unanswered questions, long before your turn. 'Am I
acceptable? Lovable? How come there's no door on the only toilet?
What time does it begin for me, the American Dream?'

Outside and down the hallway, it was so peaceful that I could
hear the echo of my heels. Workers from other government offices
55   – clean-shirted people, with keys to proper bathrooms, and mouths
that brimmed with American smiles – gathered round a coffee cart.
A door with a big judicial seal flew open, and I sprang back. A
tall white man in a baseball cap came out with a tall black man
whose hands were padlocked behind his back. Something almost
60   tender in the captor's touch on the arm of his broken-looking
prisoner reminded me of the grandma and the young man. I took
the elevator down. From the wall of the lobby, a portrait of
President Bush (Oval Office, flag) was grinning at the
undiminished crowd outside the glass doors and at a big white
sign nearby. 'Why are you waiting on this line?' it read, in many
66   languages. 'Did you know you can call (212) . . .' But the rest had
been blanked out with a sticker; from where I stood (with the
grinning man) you couldn't see any number to call at all.

Kennedy Fraser,
The New Yorker
11 January 1993

ACTIVITIES – STAGE **3**:

1 Now come back together as a class. How did you feel about reading and discussing the texts like this? Would you like to do it again? Would you like to find some texts yourselves, and bring them into class for another session like this?

2 Look at the next drawing by Mel.

- Who is this man?
- What do you think he is writing?
- Look at his three trays of papers. Trays like that usually have a word or two on them to say what they contain. Choose words to write on the trays. Think carefully about the one on the right.

ACTIVITIES – STAGE **4**:

1 Form again the two groups you worked in for the reading activity. Discuss your experiences of bureaucracy and officialdom – in your own or some other country. The student who guided your work before will be in charge, to see that all students get a chance to speak.

2 Within your groups, work out a short role-play. One of you is an official. All the others are people who need different things from the official, all of them in a desperate hurry. Act out for the other group what happens.

UNIT III

ONE: EXPLORING THE CHANGING WORLD

ACTIVITIES – STAGE 1:

1 In this Unit we are going to explore some of the ways in which our world is changing, and the language we use to talk about the changes that have already happened, what is happening now, and what is likely to happen in the future. First, look at three cartoons which appeared in *The New Yorker* magazine. With your partner, try to work out what the *subject* of each cartoon is, and then try to say in very simple English what is actually happening, not in the cartoon but in the world. For the subject, use only a word or two. To say what is happening in the world, write a complete sentence, using the present continuous tense. We have given you one example, below, which is not the subject of these cartoons.

SUBJECT	WHAT IS HAPPENING
Population increase	The number of people in the world is increasing rapidly.

"Books by men are in the basement." Donald Reilly,
The New Yorker

Ros Chast,
The New Yorker

Dedini,
The New Yorker

2 When we discuss topics like these in English, we encounter a tricky (and sometimes neglected) bit of English grammar: **countable** and **uncountable nouns**, and the **articles** (definite, indefinite) and other words (like *some* and *any, much* and *many*) that we can use with them.

First, look at this list of nouns. They may include some you have already used in this chapter. Put them into lists to show whether they are usually countable or uncountable. (We say *usually*, because, as we shall see later in this Unit, English vocabulary and even grammar are also changing.)

COUNTABLE   UNCOUNTABLE

advance

pollution

species

equality

rights

threat

identity

increase

discrimination

status

engineering

gene

wildlife

planet

environment

destruction

discovery

research

3 Just to remind yourself, look now at these words and expressions, and list them in the columns below to show which can be used with singular or plural countable nouns, which with uncountable, and which with all.

the (definite article)	*much*
a/an (indefinite article)	*many*
some	*every*
any	*little/a little*
few, a few	*a lot of*
several	*enough*
all	*most*

Countable singular	Countable plural	Uncountable	All

4 Look now at the following possible titles for a serious article or book on one of the topics covered in the cartoons, and indicate which of them is correct as it stands (put a ✓), and which would be more natural English with a definite article; for these, write the definite article in front of the title.

- Women's roles in society
- Changing status of women
- Genetic engineering
- Future of genetic engineering
- Way men see themselves
- Pollution of the environment
- Environmental pollution
- Threat to tradition from gene research
- Preservation of wildlife
- Discovery of how our genes work

– Recent advance in sexual equality
– Saving endangered species from destruction
– Sexual politics and equal rights
– Positive discrimination
– Future of our planet
– Gender identity, its past and its future

5 When you have done this, try to work out why you used *the* before some titles and not before others.

ACTIVITIES – STAGE 2:

1 Still working in pairs, think of an important way in which the world is changing, and agree it between you. Then think of a cartoon on the subject. The one of you who draws best will draw the cartoon. You may use some words in your cartoon, or in a caption under it, but try not to use too many.

2 The pairs will now exchange cartoons all over the class. Try to guess the subject of the cartoon you have been given. Then check with the pair who did the cartoon to see if you were right.

3 Now, using this cartoon, write:

– the title of a serious article or book on the subject of your cartoon
– the first sentence of the article or book.

Remember, as you work, some of the grammar we have just reviewed.

Here is an example of a title and a first sentence, based on the example given in the first exercise in this section:

POPULATION INCREASE: A THREAT TO THE FUTURE OF OUR WORLD

The number of people in the world is growing at a rate so rapid that scientists fear this increase is more than the planet can support.

4 Your teacher may ask you to complete your article as homework, and will then tell you how many words to write, probably not more than 300.

Or you may decide, as a class, on one subject of this kind that interests you all, and write about it in this style.

ACTIVITIES – STAGE **3**:

1 When we think about changes like this, we think also of what is likely to happen in the future. For this purpose, of course, we use **modals.** By now, at your level, you know how these work. To remind yourself, look at this list of some English modals, and check (✓) those that we use when we guess at future possibilities in English:

May/may not	Ought to/ought not to
Could/couldn't	Can/cannot
Might/might not	Should/shouldn't
Dare/dare not	Have to/don't have to
Must/mustn't	

2 Now underline the *three* which you think we are most likely to use when we are talking about possibilities (*not* opinions) in the future.

3 Using these three, and working with a partner, take one of the topics we have considered in this chapter, and say what you think is possible in the future. Remember to use the three modals you have picked from the group above and underlined.

ACTIVITIES – STAGE **4**:

1 Try to decide, as a class, which you think is the single most important change happening in the world today.

2 Can you, as a group, do anything to influence this change? What?

TWO: CHANGING TECHNOLOGY

ACTIVITIES – STAGE 1:

1 Here is another cartoon from *The New Yorker*. Working with a
partner, try to tell each other, briefly, the story behind it: what
happened before, what is happening in the picture, what might
happen later. Include some details of the weather, the cars, and the
thoughts of the two men. Begin 'A man was driving . . .'

"I was sad because I had no on-board fax until I saw a man who had no mobile phone."

W. Miller,
The New Yorker

2 The cartoon is about one technological change. With your
partner, write one sentence that sums up your feelings about
technological changes in your lifetime: the number of them, how
important (or unimportant) you think they are, how you feel
about them.

3 Try now to list some of these with your partner. Do not write
sentences, but simply use nouns (*fax, mobile phone*). Put them
under the headings below, to indicate which part of your life they
come into.

– Your life at home
– Your life at work or study
– Your daily transport and distant travel
– Your medical care
– Your leisure time
– Your life as a citizen of your country

ACTIVITIES – STAGE 2:

1 Now you are going to read an article from *The Independent*. Before you read, look briefly at these few words and phrases connected with telephones, to be sure you know them. You may find it helpful, working with your partner, to do a small drawing and point to parts of it.

flex	*curly flex*	*portable*	*handset*
cradle	*recharging component*	*receiver*	*unit*

2 As you read, match the sentence beginnings in column 1 with the endings in column 2.

COLUMN 1

Philip Norman . . .

The salesman . . .

Mrs Philip Norman . . .

The elderly lady on the Isle of Wight . . .

The female publicity director in New York . . .

The cat . . .

The New York publishing director . . .

COLUMN 2

. . . was horrified that anyone could leave a telephone unanswered.

. . . loved the portable telephone as though it was a favourite pet.

. . . was sick and vomited everywhere.

. . . was suspicious about the sounds coming over the telephone.

. . . had wonderful news, and couldn't understand why the reaction was not a happy one.

. . . had a fake expression, like something made of plastic, and no real interest or sympathy.

. . . was first unenthusiastic about portable telephones, but couldn't now go back to life without one.

Philip Norman on Life Without a Flex

There is a famous picture – called, I think, *A Night to Remember* –
in which a lifeboat full of distraught men and women watch with
dumb horror as the mighty hull of the *Titanic* rears up, to vanish for
ever in the cold, fathomless depths of the Atlantic. I myself have
recently suffered a similar trauma. I dropped my portable   5
telephone into the lavatory.

Though retrieved in a second, it was already beyond help. You
would never have thought that anything so seamless-looking could
instantly ship such gallons of Blue Flush-tinted water. Though I
shook and shook the drops from it, like an altar boy with his   10
censer, no sign of life remained. No trace of that small red light,
flicking on, then off, then firmly on again. Not even the faintest
echo of that soft, peripatetic purr.

At my local telephone shop, the long-haired salesman smiled
with Styrofoam sympathy. 'Makes a change,' he said. 'Mostly   15
people drop them in the bath.' I asked whether, since the cradle
and recharging component were undamaged, I could simply buy a
new receiver. 'Sorry, squire. We can only sell you the complete
handset-and-cradle unit. It's for your own protection, actually . . .'

Rather than fall for that, I resolved to manage without a portable 20
telephone. But it was like returning to the Ice Age. Ringing noises
kept breaking out in distant rooms. As I plodded to answer them, I
could almost feel shoe leather eroding. I rediscovered the meaning
of 'hang on', stuck to the wall by prehistoric curly flex when I could
simultaneously have been washing up, making coffee, opening   25
letters, receiving bike deliveries, feeding the cat or simply striding
energetically to and fro.

You will by now have recognised a pathetically late convert to
modern telephone technology. I am not by any means an old man,
but in telecommunication terms just dial M for Methuselah. When I 30
was a child, telephones were sculpted black objects standing
foursquare on hall tables and kitchen dressers, and south London
exchanges had names like Macaulay and Tulse Hill. Incoming
calls, if not bad news, were social occasions, to be shared by the
whole family ('Phil's here as well. Do you want a word with him?'). 35
Outgoing calls could not be made until three big old pennies had
been dropped into a tin moneybox shaped like a log cabin.

Then I grew up to choose a profession whose worst enemy is the
telephone. What writer in his senses works near something that at
any moment can go off like a hand grenade? To my wife's abiding   40

horror, I can ignore a ringing telephone for hours on end. 'I've been trying to reach you for days,' people sometimes complain. 'Well,' I reply pleasantly, 'now you've reached me . . .'

45   The so-called telecommunications revolution of the mid-Eighties left me unmoved. Little had changed so far as I was concerned. The line between my central London flat and my mother's, in the next street, still crackled and broke up like a bad connection to the Congo. The millions we all poured into the new monopoly seemed spent chiefly on cosmeticisation and tinkering. Metallic voices
50   informed one that five-figure numbers had now been changed to six-figure numbers, and that the time was given courtesy of Accurist. Like many others, I longed to meet the British Telecom sprite mascot on a dark night and mug it back.

     Not until a year ago did I realise how far I had been left
55   behind. Visiting an elderly lady on the Isle of Wight, I saw that even she now had a portable telephone. Comfortably stained and scuffed, it lay on her knitting-basket like a sleeping lapdog. 'I wouldn't be without it,' she said with the same devoutness my grandmother used to refer to liquid TCP.

60   Models of portable telephones have names that are implicit character statements: Lifestyle, Relate, Duet, Dallas. It seemed sensible to choose the BT Freelance, pending something more specific (the BT Biographer or the BT Belletriste?).

     Ironically, for a long time, the one place I scrupled to use my
65   portable phone was in the lavatory. I was convinced I could tell when people ringing me were so engaged, and I hesitated to give back so specific an estimate of their importance. But the moment came when, having just dialled my New York publisher to speak to two different executives, I was smitten by an irresistible urge to
70   pee. Gambling that the transatlantic connection-time would be sufficient, I wedged the phone under my chin and unzipped my fly. I had just begun when my first interlocutor, a well-bred female publicity director, suddenly spoke in my ear. I covered the mouthpiece, but too late. 'My God!' she cried. 'What is that
75   incredible noise?'

     'Tina, I'm so sorry', I said. 'I'm just washing up the cup from my afternoon tea.'

     As she rather sceptically transferred me to the publishing director, I moved back into the study with the portable phone and
80   sat on the couch, ready to discuss sales of my new book. He was just telling me the total copies sold to date when I saw my cat across the room begin to throw up extravagantly.

'It's a nice clean sell-through of the edition . . .' the cultivated American voice said in my ear as I chased the cat into the kitchen, trying to shoo her furiously while making no sound into the   85
receiver. '. . . of course, we'll be monitoring for a reprint. . .' he continued as I trapped the still-puking cat under the table, diverted her to the study and bundled her out through the security bars, finally releasing my pent-up breath in a loud gasp. 'Philip! Whatever's the matter?' the voice in my ear broke off solicitously.   90
'You sound devastated. This is really good news I'm giving you. . .'

Oh, there's never a dull moment with the BT Freelance. Especially if you forget to put the lavatory lid down.

Philip Norman,
The Independent Magazine
23 January 1993

ACTIVITIES – STAGE 3:

1 To demonstrate your understanding of the text, first form groups of four. Then look carefully at, and talk about, the scenes listed below, so that you can *mime* (act without speaking) what happens in the scenes. Then choose one student to do the mime. The rest of the class watches, identifies whether the scene is one, two or three, and says whether any action has been omitted.

Scene One: lines 5–13, 'I dropped . . . purr.'
Scene Two: lines 22–27, 'As I plodded . . . to and fro.' (*Two* different mimes in this scene.)
Scene Three: lines 78–89, 'As she rather . . . gasp.'

2 In the same groups, discuss, first, why we do *not* ask you to do a mime of the most important scene in the text, which is in lines 67-77, 'But the moment . . . my afternoon tea.'

3 Instead, please show your comprehension of the scene by choosing from the statements below the only two which are correct.

(a) Philip Norman suspected that other people had rung him from this same room, but he had never done it before.
(b) The scene took place in the kitchen.
(c) The transatlantic call took so long to connect that he was able to finish what he was doing.

(d) The sound the New York publicity director heard was a cup being washed up.
(e) He had the telephone in one hand, the cat in the other.
(f) He tried to block off the sound with his hand, but failed.

4 Here are some words from the text. Put them into the correct box, and then do what the instructions in the box say.

devastated	purr	scuffed
gasp	sprite mascot	plodded
striding	crackled	shoo

Two words for ways of walking. List some other words for ways of walking, and talk to each other about them. You may want to get up and demonstrate them to each other.

Three words that describe sounds. Which one is usually applied to a cat, which to an electronic noise, and which to a noise made by a person? Tell each other some more words you know for noises people make, other than words that mean speaking or talking.

Two words that mean the symbol of a company that looks like a fairy or spirit. Can you think of similar symbols of a company, a school, or a country?

A word that means a gesture of trying to make something move or go away. List and mime the meanings of some other words for gestures.

A word that means very upset. List one or two other words the author could have used in this place in the sentence without greatly changing the meaning.

A word that describes something like an old pair of shoes. Think of other words to describe things that have been used a lot.

5 When we are talking about changes and their results, we often use the present perfect tense. This interesting and challenging tense enables you to convey meaning without saying everything explicitly. The present perfect covers an event in the past (often, but certainly not always, the recent past) which we relate to something in the present. It is easy to see how this works when the past event is actually the cause of what happens in the present, as in this example:

Students in the class are wearing warmer clothes today, because the weather has changed.

Here is another example, based on one of the topics of this chapter.

People are no longer using the mail for urgent documents, because fax has made it possible to transmit them instantly.

First, work out a similar sentence based on something that has recently happened to you, or to the class.

6 Now, using some examples from Chapters One and Two of this Unit, list in one column some recent changes in the world, and in the other, their results. Then write sentences, or pairs of sentences, using the present perfect for the cause, the present simple or present continuous for the result.

Here is an example of what your two columns should look like, and two examples of how the sentence or sentences could be.

THE EVENT IN THE PAST WHICH CAUSED THE CHANGE	WHAT IS HAPPENING IN THE PRESENT AS A RESULT
The rapid development of computers	Fewer people employed

Examples of sentences:

Fewer people are being employed as office workers, because the rapid development of computers has made their jobs unnecessary.

The rapid development of computers has made many clerical jobs unnecessary. As a result, companies are employing fewer office workers.

THREE: THE TECHNOLOGY OF NUMBERS

ACTIVITIES – STAGE 1:

1 With your partner, see how many examples you can find of situations in which you, personally, are identified by a number. You may want to look at cards in your wallet or handbag, and to think of situations at work, when dealing with officials, or when using your own or an office computer.

2 As the world changes in this way (more and more numbers as a means of identity) what effect will this have on the way people think of themselves, and of one another?

ACTIVITIES – STAGE 2:

1 You are going to read a short poem on the subject we have been talking about. In the title, the word *Reflections* has nothing to do with mirrors – it is an uncommon word meaning careful, unhurried thoughts. Similarly, the word *Royalty* has nothing to do with kings and queens. When an author (or, in the case of this book, two authors) writes a book, he or she gets paid a certain (*very* small) amount of money for each copy of the book sold. This amount is called a royalty. So the more copies of the book (*this* book, for instance) people buy, the more the authors (in this case Ben and Mel) get paid.

What they mean is – please BUY this book

A *royalty statement* is the piece of paper the publishers send to the author, to say how much money they owe him or her.

2 As you read, please simply record with a short note what you learn about the following:

032838
027564
036040
014

Reflections on a Royalty Statement

They've given me a number
So they will know it's me
And not some other Wendy Cope
(They publish two or three).
When I go to see them   5
I wear a number-plate
Or sometimes I salute and say,
'032838.'

What a lot of authors!
The digits make it clear   10
That publishers are busy –
You can phone them once a year
But it isn't done to grumble
If the cheque's a little late:
'Look, we've other things to think about,   15
032838.'

Sometimes they give a party
And all the numbers go.
'It's 027564!'
'036040!'   20
'Hey, have you seen 014's book?
You're right. He's second-rate.
But even so he's better than
032838.'

25   We're one big happy family
      (My eyes are getting runny)
      And, what is more, if we do well
      They give us pocket-money!
      Some publishers are terrible
30   But mine are really great.
      OK? Can this go in my book? –
      032838

Wendy Cope,
Making Cocoa for Kingsley Amis

ACTIVITIES – STAGE 3:

1 Read the poem again. Identify:

(a) *they* in *They've* (line 1).

(b) the probable speaker of 'Hey ... better than 032838' (lines 21–24).

(c) the speaker of 'Look, we've other things to think about, 032838.' (lines 15–16).

2 The poem refers to publishers three times:

(a) They've . . . two or three (lines 1–4)
(b) The digits . . . a little late (lines 10–14)
(c) And, what is more . . . great (lines 27–30).

   Match each of these references, (a), (b) or (c), with these summaries of what is probably in the poet's mind as she writes.

I   Publishers pay us tiny little sums of money, like what parents give to children, but I dare not complain because the publisher will read this.
II   I have a perfectly good and unique name, so why identify me by a number as though they'd never met me?
III Publishers value their own time, but are not much bothered about delays in paying their authors.

ACTIVITIES – STAGE 4:

1 As a whole class, look carefully at these numbers:

032838   027564   036040

How do we say them in English? Which two of them, when spoken, have the same rhythm? The teacher will do this first, and then the class will do it.

2 To enjoy the poem fully, you will want to read it aloud. But before you do, try speaking the three numbers and clapping your hands in time to the rhythm. The teacher will do this first, and then the class will do it.

3 Divide into groups of four. Each student takes one of the four parts of the poem. Look at your part and go through it marking the stress on individual lines, like this:

☐   ☐

They've given me a number

☐   ☐   ☐

So they will know it's me.

4 Now, in your groups, read the poem aloud, each student reading the part he or she has marked.

ACTIVITIES – STAGE 5:

1 Look at the two numbers below. Which one is a code or identification number? Which one is a measurement or amount of something? How did you decide?

327564   327,564

2 Your teacher will remind you of the ways we write and speak numbers in English, and point out any differences from the way these are done in your language. Then, please speak these two numbers correctly.

3 In the last group of activities, (stage 4), we spoke the number *0* like the letter *o*. What other three ways can we say the number *0* in English? When would we use these other three ways? When would we simply leave out the *0* when speaking the number?

4 You know from the poem that we call an individual number a *digit* (546 is a three-digit number). When we give a number of, say, nine or more digits to someone who has to write it or type it in, we often divide it into groups of three or four. In pairs, please each write a ten-digit number, and each, in turn, dictate it to your partner. Did you get it right? How easy did you find it to write it correctly?

5 When the number is a measurement or amount, of course, we do not simply say the numbers one by one, but divide it into groups of hundreds, thousands, millions. In pairs, first write a seven-digit number which is a measurement of something (money, distance etc). Dictate it to your partner, and then the other way around. Did you do this correctly? Did you put commas in the right places?

6 Look at the number below. What do we call the (.) in the number? How do we say the number?

27.53

7 How do we say these symbols?

+   −   ×   =   @   %

8 Here are two sums of money, in English and American currencies. Write out (as you would on a cheque) the amounts.

£526.98 $143,560.50

Now choose a currency you use often, write an amount in figures (like these), then dictate it to your partner, who will write it in (English) words. Do this the other way around, and check your answers.

After all these numbers, how are you feeling?

I'm not feeling really 100% today

99%

ACTIVITIES – STAGE 6:

1 To end this chapter, we will play a game to help you practise speaking numbers correctly, naturally, and in the right rhythm. First, you may want to look back briefly at the work we did on pages 145–146, about speaking numbers correctly.

2 We are all going to a party like the one in the poem. Every student in the class will make a large, easily readable number on a piece of paper or card, and pin it on or hold it up; not more than six-digit numbers, please.

Get up and move around the room. Do the things we do at parties, but use your numbers instead of names.

Introduce yourselves, and each other. 'I'm ...' 'Do you know my friend ...?'

Comment on your names (numbers). 'I have a great friend called ... Are you related?' 'If we have a boy/girl, I'm going to name him/her ...'

Gossip about other people at the party. 'I've heard that ... is losing his job. They say that ... is seeing ...'s wife.'

Flirt with each other. 'I've always thought ... was a sexy number. I've always wanted to meet a man/woman called ...'

FOUR: THE CHANGING LANGUAGE

ACTIVITIES – STAGE 1:

1 As an advanced learner, you know that the English language is not permanent and fixed. It changes rapidly and constantly. Suggest to the class some reasons why this happens. Give one example of something that has changed since you began learning English.

2 Does your own first language change as much as English? Does this happen for similar reasons, and in similar ways?

ACTIVITIES – STAGE 2:

1 You are going to read an article from *The New Yorker* magazine, which is about language. In it you will find the word **slang**, which you probably know. Your teacher will ask you some questions about it, to be sure that you all agree on the meaning. What are the advantages and the dangers of learning the slang of a language that is not your own?

2 Look at the summary of the article below. It contains a dozen or more mistakes – not grammar mistakes, but places where the article says something different from the summary. Put a ring around the mistakes, and then correct the summary so that it gives an accurate account of what the article says.

Calvin Trillin, a young English woman, found the word *raver* in an American novel while visiting friends in New York. An older brother, she guessed, would probably have said that the word meant *ditz-brained*. From the text we also learn that English people prefer toast newly-made, fresh and moist; that American policemen are called *cagmags*, and are noted for their courtesy; that Margaret Thatcher was her country's *sitcom* for many years; and that *gormless* is a new word, first used in 1994.

Broken English

During a recent breakfast at the house of some friends in London, I was forced to ask my host, straight out, what 'gormless' meant. I had noticed that one of the English papers, in its American coverage, described MTV as 'the gormless pop video channel.'

In England, I'm constantly asking what something means. As a   5
result, reading the papers with me over breakfast is not considered a stress-free way of starting the day. Considerate American guests are expected to ask one or two initial questions at breakfast — say, about whether there is some nutritional purpose behind the English custom of drying out the toast thoroughly in one of those   10
little silver racks before eating it – and then keep a decent peace.

In my defense, I should say that I had tried to puzzle out 'gormless' for myself by tossing the root word around in a couple of forms: 'I'm impressed that MTV no longer falls back on any cheap gorming,' and 'The man is completely lacking in common   15
gorm.'

I often manage to figure out a piece of English slang without assistance. The day before, it had been obvious to me what one paper meant by referring to someone as the new 'supremo' of ITV – an English television channel that is considered at least   20
marginally less gormless than MTV. (I can pass on that information with some confidence, because my host informed me that 'gormless' means 'lacking discernment or thought' – what I believe my daughters would call ditz-brained.)

Over the years, I've had only a mild interest in the differing   25
usages that Americans have traditionally employed to make facile characterizations of the mother country. ('Where else would cops be courteous enough to refer to a lineup as an identity parade, and antique dealers be quaint enough to categorize old pitchforks as farming bygones, and restaurant proprietors be dowdy enough   30
to include on menus a vegetable dish known as mushy peas?') I do like to keep up with the new slang, though, and on my recent trip I came to realize that I'm falling behind.

Some Britishers might be falling behind themselves. My host seemed to be on shaky ground when I looked up from the paper   35
one morning and asked him to define 'raver,' which he thought of as a loud partygoer. When I asked the same question of my host's daughter, she left the impression that her father's answer had reflected a certain gormlessness. Analyzing ravers as a distinct subculture, she explained that they often go around in baggy black   40

trousers, and sometimes carry whistles, and often take the drug
Ecstasy during raves, and dance to music she doesn't happen to
care for. ('It does my head in.')

Her father had at least been on the right track. I would call him
45   slightly out of date rather than ditz-brained. On the other hand,
neither he nor anyone else in the family could identify a word I ran
across in an *Independent* piece on Sir Nicholas Fairbairn, a
Scottish Member of Parliament, who remarked that some of the
women in the House are simply 'cagmags, scrub heaps, old
50   tattles.' It was easy to get the drift of 'scrub heap'; nobody wants to
be called a heap of anything. I'm familiar with old tattles; I have
even been tattled on by a few of them. But 'cagmag'?

I figured it was a term like 'sitcom,' formed by putting together a
couple of first syllables that might have done everybody a favour
55   by remaining in their own words. I asked an assortment of
Britishers, to no avail. I consulted a dictionary of slang, but it was
silent on the subject of cagmags. As a last resort, I tried the Oxford
English Dictionary, which informed me that a cagmag is a tough
old goose – and has been, at least in parts of Yorkshire and
60   Lincolnshire, since the late eighteenth century. As far as I could
gather, the opponents of Margaret Thatcher had gone through her
entire reign as the country's supremo without that information on
hand.

While I had the O.E.D. out, I looked up 'gormless,' just on a
65   hunch. There it was – dated to 1883 in its current spelling, and to
1746 in a previous version, 'gaumless.' I found all that
discouraging. I had been having difficulty enough keeping up with
fresh English slang. Now it turns out that they're adding words
from both ends.

Calvin Trillin,
The New Yorker
23 November 1992

ACTIVITIES – STAGE 3:

1 At your stage of learning, you meet many new words. It is
   important to make decisions about whether the word is one you
   need only to understand, one you may want to use yourself, or
   one you understand in this particular text, but can then forget.
   What reasons help you to make these decisions?

2 Here are some of the slang words in the text. First, choose a
definition from the group at the bottom; some are given in the
text (though the actual words of the definition may be different),
some you should be able to guess from the text. Then (✓) one of
the three columns to indicate whether the word is one to
understand, to be able to use, or simply to forget.

Slang word	Definition	Understand	Use	Forget
gormless				
ditz-brained				
supremo				
lineup				
raver				
sitcom				
cagmag				

Definitions:

(a) A situation comedy on television.
(b) A person who goes to parties where people take drugs and
    listen to a particular kind of music.
(c) A tough old goose.
(d) The head person of an organization.
(e) Stupid.
(f) Stupid in a particular way: brainless, uninteresting, without
    imagination or excitement.
(g) A group of men or women brought together by the police so
    that a witness can identify a suspect.

3 Some of the other words in the article are also ones which, although not slang, you will want to choose whether to learn to understand, to use, or neither. Here, we give a definition, you find the word in the article, and then decide, as you did before, how to regard the word.

Definition	Word	Understand	Use	Forget
Something to put toast in				
A tool farmers use				
Slightly				
Shallow, thoughtless				
Out of date, unfashionable				
Old-fashioned in a nice, charming way				
Old in a way that makes something interesting and valuable				
A small group within a larger culture				

ACTIVITIES – STAGE 4:

1 Making judgments of this kind about words is one of the most important steps towards perfecting your English. Some students try, with each new word, to record not only spelling and pronunciation, but the register of the word: formal, informal, slang, archaic or obsolete, and so on. This may be too ambitious for you, but you should, at least, know these words for different registers. Try to match each one with its definition:

Register of word:

Colloquial

Idiomatic

Idiom (noun)

Technical

Jargon (noun)

Dialect (noun)

Humorous

Pompous

Archaic

Obsolete

Definition:

(a) Over-formal, making the speaker or writer sound self-important.
(b) Specialized to one trade, profession or kind of study.
(c) Language which is not only specialized, but unnecessarily difficult.
(d) Intended to make you laugh.
(e) Language used only in one region or by one group.
(f) Language appropriate for speech and writing between friends.
(g) A phrase widely used by native speakers of one language, but hard for speakers of other languages to understand because the individual words have a different meaning from their usual one.
(h) Typical of the way native speakers of the language speak to one another.
(i) No longer used.
(j) Very old and out-of-date.

2 The reason why this matters so much is, obviously, because you want to use words *appropriate* to a particular situation. To explore this idea of appropriacy, look back at *ditz-brained* (page 151). Write a sentence or two, using the details below, to show when, where, and by whom this word could be used in a way that would be appropriate:

– age of speaker/age of other person
– relationship (friends, relations, work colleagues)
– written, spoken, both
– situation (everyday conversation, party, funeral, business letter).

3 Now here are some other ways of expressing similar ideas. Match the words to the appropriacy guide.

APPROPRIACY GUIDE	WORDS
Two fifteen-year old boys talking about a boy they don't like.	*that stupid ass*
A government document about helping people.	*of less than average intelligence, less than three on a scale of one to twenty-five*
One woman explaining angrily to another why she stopped going out with a man they both work with.	*gormless*
A teacher talking about a pupil she likes but who is not doing well.	*a bit slow*
An English employer explaining why he is not going to promote someone.	*mentally disadvantaged*
An article in an academic publication.	*nitwit, blithering idiot, birdbrain*

ACTIVITIES – STAGE 5:

1 The article from *The New Yorker* explored some of the differences between British and American English. As a student, you should know about these differences. Here are a few examples. Try, under each of the two headings, to give one more example.

SPELLING DIFFERENCES

| **British** | *theatre* | *flavour* | *defence* |
| **American** | *theater* | *flavor* | *defense* |

VOCABULARY DIFFERENCES

| **British** | *solicitor, barrister* | *boot* (of a car) | *lorry* |
| **American** | *attorney, lawyer* | *trunk* (of a car) | *truck* |

2 The good news for students is that these differences, which once made learning English like attempting two languages at once, are fast disappearing. Part of the reason for this is technological: increased fax and computer transmissions, for instance. Another is increased mobility: companies send employees from both countries (and people like yourselves) all over the world. Still another is that films and television employ British and American actors (and those from other important English-speaking parts of the world like Australia, New Zealand, Canada, South Africa, the Caribbean and Hong Kong). Try, as a class, to give examples from your own experience of the reasons why English is turning into a language with a large central core of words, spelled and pronounced alike, which most users of the language, wherever they live, can understand.

3 There are still, of course, differences between the varieties of English that can lead to misunderstandings. As a class, discuss with your teacher whether the English you are learning is predominantly American, British, or some other. Bearing in mind differences in spelling, vocabulary, and pronunciation, is this ever likely to cause you any problems?

ACTIVITIES – STAGE **6**:

1 The language is also changing because of the introduction of new words, and by the use of older words in a new way. To help you understand what is happening, we have given you some words from a survey done in 1990 of words first recorded then. Because these are not yet in most dictionaries, we also give brief definitions. What you have to do is to look at the list of some ways in which new words are introduced, and match them with the words themselves.

acid house party: a party in a big empty building, where special music is played and drugs are used

boxers: men's boxer shorts

care card: a plastic card containing a person's medical records

clergyperson: a priest, male or female

faxphone: a device for using fax by telephone lines

to greenlight: to give permission for something to go ahead

lager lout: a (usually British) young man who gets drunk and fights

ozone-friendly: not harmful to the earth's ozone layer

sound-bite: something short and memorable said on radio or television, usually by a politician

thirtysomething (noun or adjective) in the age range from thirty to thirty-nine, or a person in that range

This word is an example of (choose one or more explanations):

(a) A word needed to cover some new technological development.
(b) A word needed to cover some new social development – something people have just begun to do, or which has just been noticed.
(c) A word newspapers have begun to use because their readers are interested in a particular subject.

(d) A word which has changed class (noun to verb, verb to noun, noun to adjective, etc).

(e) A word reflecting current PC language.

(f) A word reflecting current environmental concerns.

(g) A word covering some change in style (hair, clothes etc), or a word shortened as this change becomes more common.

(h) A word describing a group of people which has become important for economic or political reasons.

2 Try, as a class, to think of some words you have seen for the first time recently. Can you find an explanation among those in Activity 1, or can you explain, yourself, why the word has come into the language?

user-friendly.

FIVE: THE CHANGING WORLD OF POP MUSIC

ACTIVITIES – STAGE 1:

1 Nothing changes as fast as the world of pop music: the performers, the styles, the technology, and the words we use to talk about these. Performers come and go, but a surprising number last a long time. In this chapter, we are going to read three texts: about the past, about the present, and about the possible future of pop music.

Look first at a few obvious words we need to discuss the subject. If some of them seem too obvious, wait: you'll have your chance. Is there any word here you want to discuss with the teacher or the class?

album	*recording artists*	*band*
single	*tour*	*composition*
Top Ten, Twenty, Thirty	*rock*	*hit*
concert	*solo*	*Number One*

2 You, the class, probably know words about pop music which your teacher doesn't. Working in groups of four, try to choose one or two words to teach your teacher. Do this seriously, as you would expect your teacher to do: be sure of the spelling and the pronunciation, and think of ways to make the meaning clear.

Your words may be about styles of music, where and when you listen, clothes and hair styles, dancing, anything you like. They may include names of groups or songs – if you know what they mean!

ACTIVITIES – STAGE 2:

1 We have a lot of reading to do in this chapter. So we must read quickly, and concentrate on getting the main points. First, the past. We will read a text about a famous pop group, the Beatles. Working as a whole class, tell what you know about the group, and your teacher will write up some of this information: how many people, who they were, when they were most famous.

2 As you read, look for the following information. If you find it, write it down. If the information is not in the article, put an **X**.

- the date of the press conference
- the name of the new album
- the place the tour starts
- the name of Ringo's wife
- the date when the Beatles were probably most famous
- the date Ringo joined the group
- the instrument Ringo plays
- the instrument his son plays
- the number of other members of the Beatles
- the full names of the other Beatles.

Ringo Starr talks to Giles Smith about shaking off the past

Nobody operates a press conference quite like Ringo Starr. But then very few people have had his practice. It is one of the most enduring images from the days of the Beatles – the four of them in a barrage of flash-bulbs, behind a thicket of microphones, hunched at a table in some airport's back room, batting back the   5
questions from the floor. And, more often than not, it was Ringo who had the biggest bat.

'How did you find America?' 'We went to Greenland and took a left turn.' 'Do you like Beethoven?' 'Yes – especially his poems.' 'Have you any brothers?' 'My brother was an only child.' 'When   10
are you going to retire?' 'In about 10 minutes.'

He could still cut it, some 15 years later when, though the Beatles were long gone, the public would still listen to a word from Ringo. 'Do you have a message for the Eighties?' he was asked as he flew into Chicago, 'Message?' he replied. 'I'm not a post   15
office.' And last week in London, he was at it again.

Ringo Starr's British Press Conference 1992 took place in the ballroom at the Dorchester Hotel. Its purpose was to announce the release in May of a new studio album, *Time Takes Time* (his first in nearly a decade), and a European tour, beginning in July. Starr   20
posed for photographs with his son, Zak, who will be part of the touring band. After that, he walked on to the podium and said 'Good morning' in a loud honk. Then the questions began.

'Why does the tour start in Sweden?' 'Because the first date is in Gothenburg.' 'What's it like having a drummer who's your son?'   25

'Not as bad as having a son who's a drummer.' 'What instruments do you prefer when you are writing?' 'I *prefer* the violin, but I can't play it.' Quick, dry, melancholic at the edges – this could have been Ringo circa 1965. Except at one point, where his tone
30   suddenly hardened up. An Italian journalist wondered if there was any political significance in Starr's planning to play at the scene of a recent terrorist incident in Viareggio. Starr said there wasn't, but added, 'It may be a surprise to you, lady, but I'm a *musician*.'

He got a round of applause for that, though Ringo's
35   musicianship has not frequently been the first thing about him that people have jumped to celebrate. He's more familiar as the amiable side-kick, the whipping post for the other three's quips. ('It's been a pleasure working with you, Ringo,' said John Lennon during a concert, shortly after Starr had trashed the band's version
40   of 'I Wanna Be Your Man'.) The Beatles used to ration his vocals to one track per album – mostly versions of other people's songs, or special, Ringo-targeted Lennon & McCartney compositions: thus he got to sing 'Boys' on *Please Please Me*, 'Act Naturally' on *Help*, and 'What Goes On' on *Rubber Soul*, and 'Yellow Submarine' on
45   *Revolver*. ('I'd be out there in the studio singing, and it was Little Richard in *my* head, and then I would go into the playback and it sounded like Bing Crosby.')

Beside the blinding experimental achievements of the others, Starr's musical contribution looked a little piecemeal. He did,
50   though, come up with the idea of blowing bubbles in a glass of water, miked up close, during the recording of *Abbey Road's* 'Octopus's Garden' (an actual Starr composition). And it was Ringo who coined the phrase 'Hard Day's Night'. ('It's been a hard day,' he once announced. Then he noticed it was dark, and
55   added "s night'.) Nevertheless, prior to joining the Beatles, he had responded to a newspaper advertisement and applied to become a cowboy, and many have claimed that, even within, the Beatles, he was only along for the ride.

It has hardly helped his cause that one of the people who has
60   most consistently lamented Starr's lack of talent, is Ringo Starr himself. Upstairs in his suite of rooms, after the conference, this was how Ringo Starr the musician explained his craft as a drummer. 'One of my laws is: if you're going to hit them, hit the buggers. With drums you just get one chance. You might as well
65   make the mistake solid as be namby-pamby about it and hide from it. So I've always felt, whack the buggers. I don't know technical

terms. I can't do a roll. I can just about do a paradiddle. I can do flams and triplets, and that's about it for me.'

But, as he also says, 'that's all I need for the style I play.' Accomplished or otherwise, Starr is one of the few pop drummers to have pioneered a style. It's there on 'She Loves You' – the hi-hat cymbal in almost continual use ('I just kept it open and made it swishy. They all thought I was a genius for that, but it was just something I did'), the tom toms pounding away. Many could have done it better, technically speaking, but it wouldn't have been the same. 'I don't think anybody plays like I do. I was playing the new album to my son Zak, just the other day. And there's a fill on one of the tracks called 'What Goes Around' – and he said, 'Only *you* could get away with that, Dad.' And you've heard that fill probably on *Sgt Pepper*, the same sort of attitude . . .'

At which point, fists thumping away at the air, Starr demonstrated what he meant. 'It's wide open, it goes, *bom* [huge pause] b-*bom* [huge pause] b-*bom* [huge pause] bom-*pshhh*. They're known as classic Ringo fills – that's how I play, and that's what everybody loved about it.'

Giles Smith,
The Independent
16 April 1992

ACTIVITIES – STAGE 3:

1 Read the article again. Did anything make you laugh or smile? What?

2 Choose from this list words you think describe Ringo's answers to the questions. Put a tick (✓) by them.

sharp	*light*	*indirect*	*witty*
dull	*deft*	*passive*	*flat*
solemn	*clumsy*	*forthright*	*idiomatic*
direct	*formal*		

3 Below are three circles for the past, the present, and the future of Ringo Starr. Put the items listed into the correct circle. The present means the time of the article. The future contains (of course) things we can only guess at, which may happen.

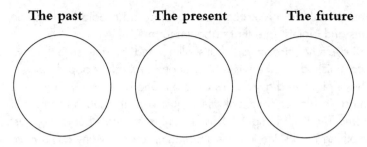

The past   **The present**   **The future**

(a) Yellow Submarine
(b) *Time Takes Time*
(c) Zak's solo concert
(d) *Sergeant Pepper*
(e) Zak's tour with Ringo
(f) Ringo tries to be a cowboy
(g) Zak's son joins the band
(h) Ringo sings 'Boys'
(i) Ringo demonstrates *bom, b-bom*
(j) Ringo in the ballroom, Dorchester Hotel, London

4 When people of Ringo Starr's age look back at the past (as in this article) they often wonder about ways in which their lives could have been different. Sometimes they express the thought in one of these structures:

> *I might have ended up as a poor man in Liverpool.*

> *I could have been a different kind of musician.*

Or they may think of one event that had a particular result, and use this structure:

> *If I had come from London instead of Liverpool,*
> *I   could   have missed the chance to be a Beatle.*
>
>   *might*
>
>   *would*

Look carefully at the grammar of these structures. Your teacher may want to review it with you. Then, using not only the text but also your imagination, explore some past possibilities, and put them into one of these structures. Use *I*, as though you were Ringo Starr. Do not limit yourself to what you know – make up as much as you like. Here are some cues to get you going:

- born earlier or later
- been a girl, not a boy
- learned the violin
- taken singing lessons
- married Brigitte Bardot
- had a daughter instead of Zak
- had eight children
- gone to a university
- born in the USA
- gone to live in New York
- met Mick Jagger instead of John Lennon
- born in India
- written more famous songs

ACTIVITIES – STAGE 4:

1 Now we are going to read an article by Louise Gray from *The Times* about something happening in the *present* to pop music.

(a) When you listen to pop music in English, how much of the language do you understand?
(b) Do you imagine that native English speakers hear and understand every word?
(c) Does listening increase your knowledge of English?

2 As you read the text quickly, match the items in list A with those in list B:

LIST A	LIST B
Catch the Word	Song by Sophie B. Hawkins
Pop Words	Translates pop songs from English into other languages
Oh Carolina	
Shaggy	Jamaican-born ragga singer
Carolina	small furry animal that lives in trees
squirrel	Shaggy's girlfriend
Damn! I wish I was your lover	A Number One hit by Shaggy
	Explains the English words of pop songs and teaches listeners how to understand them

At Bush House, the headquarters of the BBC's World Service radio, English language is a serious business. The howls of laughter emanating from a dimly-lit basement cutting room are proof of this. Here, a producer is splicing together out-takes from an edition of *Catch The Word*, a programme that translates English-language pop songs into any of more than 25 languages.

On this occasion, the intricacies of the Beatle's 'Ob-la-di, Ob-la-da' are being translated into Castilian Spanish, much to the mirth of the woman entrusted with the task. 'Desmond says to Molly: "Girl, I like your face",' Paul McCartney sings. 'Desmond has an odd way of expressing his love,' deadpans the programme's co-presenter. An explosion of laughter is followed by a click as the producer's razor-blade falls.

For a handful of the 130 million people who regularly tune in to the World Service, the station will always be the last redoubt of pukka English, where each spoken word shimmers under the enunciation that empire intended. But for more than five and a half million teenagers worldwide who tune in to *Catch The Word* and another programme, *Pop Words*, English has a more prosaic use: to encourage fluency in the international language of pop.

Compiled by the BBC's English Service, which this year celebrates its 50th anniversary, *Pop Words*, is a 15 minute show that uses hit songs to explain the vagaries of idiomatic English. Every week, presenter David Evans and his producer, Keith Ricketts, take a current pop song and painstakingly examine it, line by line. Works to have come under the microscope have included hits by Meat Loaf, Whitney Houston and Shaggy's ragga No. 1, 'Oh, Carolina'.

'Carolina! Wind your body, girl! Mek 'em know that you have it in you to mad 'em,' rasps the Jamaican-born Shaggy. An American voice repeats his words in full Jamaican dialect.

'What's he saying? What's happening?' Evans asks. 'He's saying: 'Carolina' – that's his girlfriend – 'come on, dance! Make the men *crazeeee!*'

That's the easy bit. A few lines further on, Shaggy waxes lyrical about Carolina's body. She moves, he declares, 'just like a squirrel'. 'A squirrel is a small furry animal that lives in trees,' Evans informs his unseen audience of millions. So does Carolina run up and down trees? Store nuts in her cheeks? Er, no. 'Shaggy is saying that he likes the way Carolina dances.' Evans says. These are not, he adds off-air, definitive interpretations.

'But we still have difficulties. I once had a very tricky song called 'Damn! I Wish I Was Your Lover', by Sophie B. Hawkins. It's got a lot of jungle imagery and there's a line that goes something like – 'I'll be your monkey/Let me come inside your jungle book.' That   45 one got us a letter from an expatriate in Zimbabwe saying we were corrupting the morals of the young.'

Of course, what is acceptable in Britain may offend listeners in other parts of the world, and Norbrook says the programme treads carefully in its choice of songs. A modicum of sex is allowable, but   50 drugs and the truly weird are definitely out.

Louise Gray,
The Times
28 January 1994

3 Match the word or phrase with its probable meaning in this text:

intricacies	A certain small amount – not too much
pukka	Word-pictures of things you find in,
vagaries	for example, a tropical rain forest
prosaic	Good, of high quality
come under the microscope	Down-to-earth, everyday
definitive interpretations	Complicated meanings
jungle images	Be looked at closely
modicum	Serious and final statements of what something means
	Unusual or unexpected ideas and acts

4 Working fast, find the following in the text.

(a) The size of the audience for the two programmes.

(b) The length of time of each programme of *Pop Words*.

(c) What Shaggy means when he says Carolina is like a squirrel.

(d) The song with a lot of jungle imagery.

(e) One thing the producers of the programmes can talk about a little, two things they have to avoid.

ACTIVITIES – STAGE 5:

1 Now, finally in this chapter, we are going to read a text by Jim White in *The Independent*. This text, by telling you what has happened in the past, and what is happening now, suggests some great changes in the future of pop music, especially of British pop music. Before you read, talk briefly with a partner about what you think the future of British pop music might be.

2 As you read the text, try to complete the diagram below, showing the success of British pop music in other countries. The chart starts in 1955, when British pop music was almost unknown outside England, and we have drawn a line to show you the way to start. Thinking of the text on Ringo Starr, and your own knowledge, draw a line to show the popularity of British pop music, and where you think it will go in the future.

1955   1960   1965   1970   1975   1980   1985   1990   1995   2000   ?

The British aren't coming. Last week when our pop industry purred through the Brit Awards, its annual bout of televised self-importance, there was only one British single in the American Top 30: Rod Stewart and Sting helping the Canadian Bryan Adams groan his way through 'All for Love'. Meanwhile the highest placed British album in *Billboard's* top 50 was Rod Stewart's

5

Unplugged and Unseated – not exactly suffering from vertigo at number 43.

Figures released this week underline the sense of decline: the estimated share of worldwide record sales by UK artists fell from 25 per cent in 1985 to 15 per cent in 1993. Remember the British motor-cycle industry? The British film industry? British industry? It can't be happening again, can it?

Pop music has been a buoyant export earner for Britain for 30 years. The Beatles, the Rolling Stones, Elton John, Culture Club and Duran Duran cut the balance of payments deficit by millions. British record company earnings are still enormous – £2bn last year. But the proportion earned abroad is falling. Worse, like the British car industry in the Seventies, our best-selling models overseas are approaching obsolescence: the Clapton, the John, the Collins, the Stewart. The most recent new product that had any serious sales abroad was the Michael in 1988, and it is presently off the road undergoing a complete overhaul.

'People had grown accustomed to the fact that since the Beatles, Brit artists had dominated the white rock field throughout the world,' says Paul Gambaccini, editor of the *Guinness British Book of Hit Singles*. 'Some of us thought as long ago as the mid-Eighties that there was no reason why it would always be so. Even then the decline has proven more swift than even I had considered.'

Meanwhile in Europe, a market traditionally gorged on British and American staples, local acts are accounting for a bigger share of their home turf. Musicians no longer feel obliged to sing in English. In Germany, the growing mood of nationalism is manifested in German lyrics being more prominent in the charts. And it is no longer laughable for Europeans to export their talents to Britain: Dutch, Swedes and Icelanders frequently infiltrate our Top 20, calling themselves 2 Unlimited, Ace of Base or Björk and proving as adept with computers as British recording artists.

Developing countries with no history of infatuation with the English language – Mexico, South Korea and Taiwan – are now among the top 15 most valuable markets. Even the Japanese, the second biggest record market in the world and traditional supporters of anything past-it and British, are discovering other voices.

Jim White,
The Independent
23 February 1994

ACTIVITIES – STAGE 6:

1 Compare your chart with your partner's. Which of you sees the brightest future for British pop music?

2 Underline, or if you normally use a coloured pen or highlighter as you read, mark these parts of the text, and put the correct letter beside them in the margin.

  (a) An example of a famous British singer now near the bottom of one list of fifty hit records.
  (b) A list of some older singers and groups who earned a lot of money for Britain.
  (c) A list of singers Jim White compares with once-famous, now out-of-date British cars.
  (d) An example of one country now beginning to prefer recording artists singing in their language, not English.
  (e) A list of non-English-speaking countries now beginning to sell records successfully in England.
  (f) A list of countries which have never been great fans of English pop music.
  (g) An example of a country which buys a lot of records, once mainly British, now less so.

3 Cover up the text, or close your book. Just from memory, try to do these with a partner.

  – See how many pop singers or groups mentioned in the text you can recall.
  – See how many countries mentioned in the text you can recall, and how much you can remember of what the text said about them.

4 Still without looking back at the text, read this summary of what it says, and fill in the missing words. These need not be the actual words used in the text, but any which are correct English and which reflect what the text says: only *one* word in each space.

There was only one British single in the recent Top Thirty, and that was _____ Canadian. The highest-placed British artist in the Top Fifty was Rod Stewart, and _____ that was _____ very high, at Number Forty-Three. British record companies _____ earn two billion pounds a year, but the _____ earned in other countries is _____. Some experts thought as _____ ago as the mid-eighties that there was no _____ why British artists should _____ the whole white rock _____ throughout the _____. In Europe, which _____ bought a lot of British records, musicians no longer feel _____ to sing in English, and they are also beginning to _____ their records to England.

ACTIVITIES – STAGE 7:

1 When we predict (guess what is going to happen in) the future, we often use what grammar books call the *future tense*. (We have many other ways of talking about the future in English.) Make six predictions about the future of pop music, using this tense, which has an easy pattern to follow: *he/she/it/they* will + infinitive without *to*. Include some predictions about individual artists, about countries, about kinds of pop music you particularly like or dislike. Here are a couple of beginnings for you to finish; then make some predictions of your own.

Madonna will . . .

British pop music will . . .

2 Your teacher probably does listening comprehension work with your class using pop songs. This chapter is a good time to use a tape, chosen either by your teacher or by you. We cannot suggest exactly what you do, because the copyright laws of your country may limit this. There are many possibilities: filling in blanks, listening for key words, putting jumbled lines into the correct order. You may be more ambitious, if your school has a camera, and make your own pop video of a song the class chooses.

3 To finish this chapter, divide the class into groups of four to six
students. In these groups, compare your own experience of music
with those of other students.

Talk about some of the following.

- Do you play any instrument? Are you learning any instrument?
- Do you like classical music as well as, or instead of, pop music?
- Does your country have a particular tradition of music? What
  words, in English, would you use to explain the native music of
  your country to people from other countries?
- If you were left on a desert island with only *one* record, which
  record would you take?

SIX: CHANGING STYLES

ACTIVITIES – STAGE 1:

1 When you brushed, combed, or whatever you did to your hair this morning, did you think about it at all? Wish it was different? Think you might change it? With a partner, talk about exactly why your hair is the way it is: because you never think about it, because all your friends do the same thing, because your parents taught you to do it this way, or some other reason.

2 We are going to read a short article by John Updike, one of the most famous American novelists. He was born in 1932. As well as his novels, he writes poems and short stories, often for *The New Yorker*. This article was published there, and is called *Hostile Haircuts*. If anyone is unsure of the meaning of *hostile*, discuss this: it is an important word in the article, and you want to get its exact meaning. From Updike's age, the title, and from these drawings (by Maurice Vellecoop) which were published with the article, try to guess what the article will be about.

3 As you read, do two things.

(a) Decide how accurate your guess about this article was;

(b) Try to summarize the article in one sentence. Do not use the word *hostile*. Begin: John Updike feels that the haircuts he sees around him . . .

Hostile Haircuts

Now that I am sixty, I see why the idea of elder wisdom has
passed from currency. My thoughts have become not only fewer
and smaller but more spiteful and timorous. The impression has
been growing upon me that I am surrounded by hostile haircuts.
5   When African-American males first began to cut their hair in skullcapping muffins sharply differentiated from shaved sides
sometimes ornamented with 'X's and other brandlike symbols, I
assumed that, within a long history of experimentation that ranged
from conking to the Afro, an intraracial code was being playfully
10   augmented, with no special message for me. When young white
men took up the same style, however, menace began to emanate
as surely as from a crowd of Marine crewcuts or F.B.I.-style tight
trims. Prior to 1960, now that I think upon it, all men's haircuts
expressed a slight hostility, a simmer of close-clipped individual
15   militance, whose subtext was 'Don't mess with [muss] me.' On the
distaff side, those lacquered hairdos from forties Hollywood were
as virginity-defensive as iron chastity belts; the height of
untouchability was reached with the beehive, which abruptly
collapsed into the limp ironed hair of the counterculture, signalling
20   a state of stoned acquiescence.
Honestly, I don't recall feeling especially threatened by sixties long
hair, at least not after my sons, still cherubically freckle-faced,
adopted it. True, some male faces, wearing a scruffy mat down to
the shoulders, with a beard thrown in for good measure, appeared
25   the opposite of pacified. Wasn't facial hair, the evolutionists
argued, a trait worth preserving, because men could scare each
other with it in battle? My main sensation of the long-hair era,
however, was the disconcerting sexual confusion of being unable
to gender-identify an attractive figure from the back, as it sashayed
30   along with locks flowing down to its hips. Now, seeing a young
male whose ostentatiously leonine hair has been cropped on the
sides in what I think of as normal fashion but is encouraged to
cascade in a Samsonesque mane down over his nape, I have no
trouble recognizing hostility.
35   When the sweet-mannered bespectacled young woman at the
local library shaved off all her hair but a tuft she dyed cerise, I
rather desperately tried to believe she was not out to get me. She
continued to twinkle behind her glasses, and to stamp the due
date. The seventies Mohawk, after all, had been somewhat
40   defused by splashes of color, its fierce statement removed to a

theatrical realm of outrageous costume. In the movie 'The Last of the Mohicans', I am assured in these very pages, Daniel Day-Lewis sports a 'really terrific head of hair . . . rock-star hair . . . greasy enough to shine with rebel integrity, yet not so disgusting that we start wondering what Hawkeye smells like.' Native American 45 haircuts (hostile to white invaders and swindlers) are a grease layer's thickness removed from rocker haircuts (hostile to family values, bourgeois repression, and regular hours). English punk haircuts (hostile to the upper class and fans of foreign soccer teams) are to be distinguished from American punk haircuts (hostile 50 to Mom, Dad, and high-school dress codes). One day, the young woman wore a bandanna over her cerise topknot, meaning either that the head librarian had spoken sternly to her or that she was experimenting with degrees of hostility, as Venetian blinds experiment with degrees of sunlight. 55

Not all haircuts are hostile in the same way. Sinéad O'Connor's is screamingly, overtly hostile, for instance, whereas Ross Perot may even think his is friendly. Ted Koppel's swooping bang is slyly but purposefully hostile – a shield of hair interposed to protect his frontal lobes from insidious waves of interviewee charm and 60 blather. Bill Clinton's hair, closely modelled on the opossum fur of his beloved Arkansas, manages to say yes and no to hostility at once, appearing both cuddly and spiky, and, in any case, composed of an unidentifiable salt-and-pepper substance, like mark-proof carpeting. It's a hairily cruel world, I've decided. Snip 65 or be snipped. We're all butting for psychological space, and leading with our warheads.

John Updike,
The New Yorker
2 November 1992

ACTIVITIES – STAGE 2:

1 The drawings are not exact illustrations of the haircuts described in the article, but some of them are certainly in the same general style. Here are some of the haircuts mentioned. Can you match them with particular drawings?

(a) The Afro
(b) Skullcapping muffins sharply differentiated from shaved sides sometimes ornamented with 'X's and other brandlike symbols

(c) Lacquered hairdos from forties Hollywood.
(d) The beehive
(e) The limp ironed hair of the counterculture (sixties long hair)
(f) Young woman . . . shaved off all her hair but a tuft she dyed cerise
(g) Marine crewcuts
(h) Rocker haircuts
(i) FBI-style tight trims
(j) Punk haircuts
(k) A young male whose ostentatiously leonine hair has been cropped on the sides . . . but encouraged to cascade in a Samsonesque mane down over his nape

2 Can you think of names for the drawn haircuts which we have not already mentioned in Activity 1, above, or better names for some of those we have mentioned?

3 Here are things that some of the haircuts mentioned may be saying, put in simpler words than those in the article. Find the haircut, and look carefully at the skilful, witty words in the article which John Updike uses about them. Then match his words with these simple versions of what the haircuts say.

(a) 'Stay away from me – I'm tough and I'll hit anybody who even touches me.'
(b) 'I'm so full of drugs that I'll say *yes* to anything.'
(c) 'I'm not called an Indian, I don't like your pale skin, and I suspect you're out to cheat me.'
(d) 'I do what I like at what time I like, and you can keep your middle-class ideas to yourself.'
(e) 'I don't look up to anybody, and your team is no good – we invented the game.'
(f) 'My parents know nothing, and I'm not going to dress or act like the other kids at my school.'

4 Choose one of the haircuts mentioned in the article, and write in a similar way what you think the haircut is saying.

5 As you would expect of one of America's most distinguished novelists, Updike's language is rich and full of meaning. Here are some passages, and some ways of exploring their richness. Your teacher may want to find other passages, and suggest other ways.

. . . All men's haircuts expressed a slight hostility, a simmer of close-clipped individual militance, whose subtext was 'Don't mess with [muss] me.'

- What is the exact meaning of *simmer*, and why does Updike use it here?
- *Muss* is a slang word used by rough, tough American men. It means something similar to *mess*, but it also has a separate meaning; to disturb someone's hair. Why does John Updike put it into this sentence?

. . . A young male whose ostentatiously leonine hair has been cropped on the sides in what I think of as normal fashion but is encouraged to cascade in a Samsonesque mane down over his nape.

- What animal is suggested by *leonine*? What other word refers to a part of the same animal?
- What person from the Bible is mentioned (in an adjective), and why is he appropriate here?

. . . She was experimenting with degrees of hostility, as Venetian blinds experiment with degrees of sunlight.

- Why do people put Venetian blinds on their windows?
- Why does Updike mention them? Where else in the article do we get the idea that the librarian is not a hundred per cent hostile?

6 Go through the article carefully looking for words which describe not hairstyles (like Mohawk or punk) but simply things that people can do with their hair (like *tight trims*, for example). First, discuss as a class any of these words whose meanings you are not sure about.

7 Now, with a partner, imagine you are going to the hairdresser. Give your partner careful directions of exactly what you want done to your hair. Your partner will do the same to you. Without talking any more about it, or letting your partner see as you work, do a drawing of the hairstyle your partner has asked for. Then compare your drawings, and decide whether the drawings show the hairstyles you hoped for.

ACTIVITIES – STAGE **3**:

1 In an earlier chapter, we discussed what clothes say about the people who wear them. In this one, we have considered haircuts in the same way. These, together with some of the other things mentioned in the article (like spectacles) or shown in the drawings (like earrings) all add up to *style*. What are some other things that contribute to a person's *style*?

2 Has the style of most people in your age group, in your country, changed in your lifetime? Has your own personal style changed recently?

3 In the article, John Updike looked back over the changing styles in his lifetime. We will now look ahead, at what your own personal style might be in the future. First, decide as a class whether you want to picture yourself in ten, twenty or thirty years from now. Then, look at the grammar we need to talk about this.

When we are describing someone as he is today, we say:

He *has* short hair.   He *is wearing* jeans and a T-shirt.

(Simple present tense)   (Present continuous tense)

To project these into the future, we say . . .

In ten years' time he *will have*   He *will be wearing* jeans and a
short hair.   T-shirt.

(Future tense)   (Future continuous tense)

4 Now picture yourself in the future. Try to describe your style then in about six sentences. Below are some possible beginnings for your sentences, and some hints to help you with them.

Possible beginnings:

In ten years' time . . .

Ten years from now . . .

Ten years from today . . .

Hints:

I will have . . . (hair)   I will be wearing . . .

   be . . .   carrying . . . (a baby, a
   weigh . . .   briefcase, six children)
   look . . .   driving . . .
                                        pushing . . .

5 Compare your word-pictures, either in groups of four, or as a whole class. Do you think you will recognize one another?

SEVEN: THE CHANGING ROLES OF MEN AND WOMEN

ACTIVITIES – STAGE 1:

1 In the last chapter we discussed *style*. Now we want to consider a word used a lot in English-speaking countries: *lifestyle*. The word will not be in older dictionaries, certainly not bilingual ones. What do you think *lifestyle* might include, in addition to things like clothes and hair that are part of style?

2 Did you mention, as part of your discussion, the roles of men and women, and the way these are changing? In your own experience, are women doing many things once only men did, and the other way around? (You may remember that we discussed this in Unit I.)

3 Many newspapers and magazines have a lifestyle section. What subjects do you think you would find in this section?

ACTIVITIES – STAGE 2:

1 We are going to read part of a text from *The Independent* by Ruth Picardie. It appeared on a page headed *Living*. She assumes her readers have heard of the idea of the New Man, and her article is about the Newish Man. Probably some students in the class can explain what a New Man is. If not, the class should guess what sort of a man he is, what he does that is new, and whether such people are real or invented by journalists.

2 It will help you to read more efficiently (and to write well yourself) if you understand how a good example of journalism like this is organized, and what it is trying to do. As you read, do two things. First, choose which of these descriptions best fits this text.

(a) It is like a leader or editorial, giving the opinion of the newspaper on some important current topic.

(b) It is a news story, which begins by giving us the facts about some significant happening, and then more details.

(c) It is a feature article, using some recent event as a way of introducing an entertaining discussion of a topic readers will be interested in.

(d) It is a piece of humorous writing, with no purpose but to make readers laugh.

3 Also, as you read, put these elements in the text in the order in which they come *in the writing*: not necessarily the same order in which they happened.

(a) A summary of the evidence that the Newish Man does exist, and the journalist's opinions about him.

(b) A review of some of the earlier ideas of other social groups similar to the Newish Man.

(c) Ruth Picardie's own experience of shared domestic work.

(d) A description of the *Men 2000* lifestyle report published by Mintel, and what it says.

(e) Ruth Picardie's account of what her women and men friends think about the subject.

The yuppie, the dinkie, the post-feminist, the slacker, the Newish Man . . . social tribes have long been a favourite with market research companies, ad agencies and journalists. Sociologists say they are an attempt to make sense of the post-industrial, post-modern world, in which the traditional alphabet of social class is   5
obsolete. Cynics say they help pay the rent: lager manufacturers are suckers for niche marketing; lifestyle pages need to be filled.

Already this month we have had the Babe Feminist, defined in the *Evening Standard* as 'the new breed of women's libbers – self-assured, sexy, delighted to wear lipstick and silk lingerie'.   10

Now comes the Newish (not to be confused with Jewish) Man, a spin-off from the *Men 2000* lifestyle report, published by Mintel at a smacking £795.

'Mintel asked 1,576 men and women how they divided the everyday household chores of grocery shopping planning,   15
cooking and laundry,' says the press release. 'By including the

men who say they are wholly or mainly responsible for just one of these tasks, Mintel was able to find "Newish Man". Nearly one in five men (18 per cent) qualified for this title.'

20   The Newish Man is contrasted with the more numerous but less snazzily-titled Semi-Sharer, who sort of helps (32 per cent), and Sloth, who does nothing at all (50 per cent). And the New Man? Since only a negligible proportion took total or equal responsibility for household tasks, he has officially been given the push.

25   There are several definitional problems with the Newish Man and his shared tasks. Ironing, I accept, is a bore. And when it comes to the kitchen, few men have got beyond spag bol and oven chips. But why include 'grocery shopping planning' as a defining domestic experience? I've never met anyone who felt that
30   drawing up a shopping list was a major chore, at least compared to that crucible of angst, *cleaning*.

In my house, the cleaning arguments centre around bleach (must be the thick sort). I insist that the kitchen cloth should be bleached at regular (OK then, daily) intervals, to stop it going
35   slimy; according to my partner, this is a sign of deep neurosis and the source of much pointless squabbling.

My experience about cleaning was borne out in a highly unscientific survey of friends and colleagues. 'She's terrible on cleanliness,' says Jeremy, 33. 'I urge her to do more. The place
40   gets more and more of a tip until we have an argument and then it gets done.'

'I sent him to the launderette because it's a self-contained task,' says Linda, 27. 'I can't trust him to spend an hour and a half cleaning the house. It wouldn't occur to him that some things were
45   dirty. And he has an ideological objection to employing a cleaner. We have endless arguments about it.'

'I would quite like to clear the car out occasionally,' says Kevin, 35. 'But she thinks there's something suspicious and suburban about it.'

50   The other problem with Newish Men is perception: he claims to take on a chore, but does his spouse verify this? 'Of course, the concept of "equal" sharing is a subjective one,' continues the press release, 'and it is revealing that, while more than four in 10 married men in Mintel's sample feel their contribution to at least
55   one of the three tasks is equal to that of their partner, only around a quarter of married women are of the same opinion.'

It may be, therefore, that the Newish Man is merely a boastful Sloth. This possibility was confirmed by my research. 'How many lies has he told you?' asks Andrea, 32, whose husband Jeremy had claimed his wife was 'terrible on cleanliness'.   60

Despite these quibbles, I believe the Newish Man does represent something significant in the development of domestic relations. The Newish Man rings true in Nineties Britain: trying to be fair in a half-hearted way, in contrast to the excess of the Eighties and the evangelism of America.   65

Ruth Picardie,
The Independent
25 February 1994

ACTIVITIES – STAGE 3:

1 As you read the text again, choose the alternative you think best reflects Ruth Picardie's opinion.

Categories like yuppie, dinkie, etc . . .
(a) are important sociological distinctions;
(b) are useful to companies selling products and editors filling space, but are not to be taken too seriously.

The Mintel *Men 2000* report . . .
(a) is expensive but contains some interesting information;
(b) includes some important new information such as the contribution men, with their greater managerial experience, make to grocery shopping planning.

Cleaning the house . . .
(a) is the worst job, and the most likely to cause problems;
(b) is the job men take up most enthusiastically.

Men's own perception of what they do in the house . . .
(a) is proved by the Mintel report to be accurate;
(b) is not supported by the women who live with them.

2 Match the terms used in the article with the (imaginary) people.

(a)	Yuppie (young urban professional)	I	Jim and Linda live in London; he is twenty-eight, she is twenty-five; he is an accountant, she is a lawyer; they have one child, Susan.
(b)	Dinkie (double income – no kids)		
(c)	Post-feminist		
(d)	Babe Feminist	II	Simon helps with the housework when he feels like it.
(e)	New Man		
(f)	Newish Man		
(g)	Semi-sharer	III	Rachel and Hugh are both forty-five, and have no children; both are merchant bankers.
(h)	Sloth		

IV   Jake does no housework of any kind.

V   Janet's lips are bright red, her underwear is expensive, she says what she thinks and she likes men.

VI   Jonathan genuinely shares all the housework with his partner, is competent and really enjoys it.

VII   Caroline thinks the original feminist ideas in America were exaggerated; she is a feminist, but more moderate and sensible.

VIII Frank shares some of the housework, but much less than he thinks and says he does.

3 Words like *yuppie* and *dinkie* are called **acronyms**: they are made from the first letters of the words they represent (often with an extra -*ie* on the end). Here are two more, from a survey of new words in the English language:

Yeepie: Youthful energetic elderly person.

Yummie: Young upwardly-mobile Muslim.

(Some definitions of *Yuppie* say the *u* is not for *urban* but *upwardly-mobile*, someone from a lower social class moving into a higher one.)

With your partner, construct an acronym *in English* for some group in your country. You can see how the grammar works: adjective + adjective (three or more) + noun. You must include one word beginning with a vowel – otherwise we can't pronounce your acronym.

The pairs then put their acronyms on the board, and the class guesses what they mean.

4 Here (number one in the list below) is one of the housework jobs mentioned in the text. First, find the others. Then, with your partner, add some jobs you know have to be done. Don't stop until you have a list of twenty.

1	Ironing	11	
2		12	
3		13	
4		14	
5		15	
6		16	
7		17	
8		18	
9		19	
10		20	

To help you to get to twenty, here are some reminders of rooms and other areas that involve work.

The kitchen
The bathroom
The bedroom
The garage
The garden
The shops
The school (if you have children)

5 Now, please divide the class into men and women. The men count up truthfully how many of these jobs they do. The women report on some man they know well: husband, boyfriend, father, brother. Rate yourself, or the men you know, on this scale.

20   New Man
15+   Newish Man
10+   Semi-sharer
0–10   Old Man
0   Sloth

6 Does the Newish Man really exist in your country?

ACTIVITIES – STAGE 4:

1 Now we are at the end of this chapter and of the book! We have been working with changes in the world. No doubt you have plans for changes in your life, too. We will end by talking together about these.

2 First, let us make some predictions for the future of this changing world. Look back briefly at some of the subjects in Unit III. Then, in groups of four, work out some predictions. For this purpose, as we have seen already, we use what grammar books call the future tense. Here are a couple of examples:

Men will do more of the housework, and women less.

Men will take a larger part in bringing up children.

3 When we talk about our own plans for the future, we rarely use the future tense, and only in special cases. We are more likely to say something like this:

I'm going to help my wife more, and spend more time with my children.

I'm starting my new job in Singapore next month, and I'm flying there on the twenty fifth.

What is the difference between the *going to* form and the use of the present continuous form for the future? Which one indicates that I have made serious arrangements, difficult to change, and which one more of a plan or intention?

4 Now prepare to tell your partner some of your plans for the future. Try to make a clear distinction between those things you have actually arranged to do, and those you only hope or intend to do.

5 When friends tell us their plans for the future, we don't usually sit in stony silence, but answer them, by saying things like:

I hope things work out well.

That sounds like a wonderful idea.

Try, in pairs, to give a natural response when your partner reports plans.

6 Teachers are human, too, and have plans. Perhaps your teacher will tell you some. Respond to these, too.

Here is one possible response to someone's plans for the future:

Good luck!

KEY TO ACTIVITIES

Many of the activities in this book are not designed to elicit answers, but to generate discussion, drawing, information exchange and so on. For these the answer key says NA, No Answer. Others are activities where many answers are possible. For these, the answer key provides Sample Answers, marked SA.

UNIT I

CHAPTER **ONE** (3)

ACTIVITIES – STAGE **1**
1 NA

2 NA

3 NA

ACTIVITIES – STAGE **2**
1 NA

2 NA

3 NA

ACTIVITIES – STAGE **3**
1 SA: In common: live in England, but feel outside of it
Differences:

MEL
English
born London
shortish
married, divorced

BEN
American and English
born Birmingham, Alabama
tall
single

ACTIVITIES – STAGE **4**
1 NA

2 (a) A *porter* does unskilled work in hospitals, like pushing patients around in wheel-chairs.
  (b) *volatile* means quickly changing in mood and feelings.
  (c) enjoy

3 The topic sentences are the first two in the paragraph.

4 NA

CHAPTER **TWO** (9)

ACTIVITIES – STAGE **1**
1 NA

ACTIVITIES – STAGE **2**
1 SA: Fritz: vain, proud, style-conscious
Sally: unexpected, original, likes expensive things

2 SA:

Mistake
Doesn't go (line 12)
A lousy English (line 17)
Eventually (line 21): check this word in your dictionary
Half of an hour (line 36)

Correct
Doesn't work
No *a*
Half an hour

3 Drawled: (b)
Exclaimed (line 50): said suddenly, often loudly, with strong feeling
Cooed (line 59): said low and softly, like the sound a dove or pigeon makes

ACTIVITIES – STAGE **3**
1 Sally is a *pretty, young English* girl.
SA: Fritz is an *overdressed, hospitable dark* German.
Christopher is an *intelligent, well-educated, young* Englishman.

2

Fritz	always	invited
Subject	*Adverb of frequency*	*Verb*
you	to black coffee.	
Object	*Preposition phrase expanding the meaning of the verb*	

3 NA

CHAPTER **THREE**   (14)

ACTIVITIES – STAGE 1

1 NA

2 NA

ACTIVITIES – STAGE 2

1 NA

2 NA

ACTIVITIES – STAGE 3

1 Miles Kington's lies: he didn't mention all the forms of exercise he takes playing with his son, listed in the last paragraph (lines 58–62).

ACTIVITIES – STAGE 4

1 (a) A full-blown doctor-patient ongoing healing relationship situation (line 11).
   (b) Ingest (line 17)
   (c) Thwacked (line 48)
   (d) Swish (line 47)
   (e) Groaning (line 49)

2 NA

3 NA

4 NA

CHAPTER **FOUR**   (20)

ACTIVITIES – STAGE 1

1 NA

2 NA

3 NA

4 NA

5 (a) Examples:
   Skin colour or race: African-American, Asian-American, person of color/non-color
   Physical type or shape: larger-than-average citizen
   Physical condition or ability: aurally inconvenienced, differently abled
   Financial position: differently advantaged
   Age: chronologically gifted
   Sex: womyn, person of gender
   (b) NA

ACTIVITIES – STAGE 2

1 NA

2 NA

3 Examples:
   Postman = postwoman, postperson
   Salesman = saleswoman, salesperson
   Chairman = chair

4 NA

ACTIVITIES – STAGE 3

1 NA

2 *Mural* A painting on a wall
   Portrait A painting of a real person or animal
   Trompe l'oeil A painting which looks so real you forget it is a painting

ACTIVITIES – STAGE 4

1 NA

2 T
   T
   F
   F
   F
   T

CHAPTER **FIVE**   (29)

ACTIVITIES – STAGE **1**

1 NA

2 SA:
  (a) Nurses, soldiers
  (b) Formal occasions, religious
       ceremonies

3 NA

4 NA

ACTIVITIES – STAGE **2**

1 In Mel's drawing the woman's
hat is like a plant; in Shaw's letter
it is a bird.

ACTIVITIES – STAGE **3**

1 Group 2
2

Tells men what clothes they must wear	Regulates the dress of its male patrons (line 2)
Robs you of the fun of choosing what to wear	Reduces to a formula a very vital human habit which should be the subject of constant experiment and active private enterprise (lines 19–20)
Behaved well in ways not mentioned in the rules	Voluntarily added many graces of conduct as to which the management made no stipulation whatever (lines 26–27)
Complained to the salesperson who sold her the hat	Soundly rated the tradesman who imposed the disgusting head-dress on her (lines 53–54)
Makes normal people feel ill	Produces a sensation of physical sickness in persons of normal humane sensibility (lines 64–65)

ACTIVITIES – STAGE **4**

1 SA:
Could I ask if you would be kind
enough to take off your hat?

I'm awfully sorry, but your hat
makes it impossible for me to see
the stage. Would you mind
removing it?

2 NA

ACTIVITIES – STAGE **5**

1 NA

2 *The Times*, 1 Virginia Street,
London E1 9XN

ACTIVITIES – STAGE **6**

1 SA:
FORMAL
suit MF
tie M
jewellery M(?) F
dinner jacket M
linen jacket M F(?)
blouse F
blazer M
bow tie M
button-down shirt M

CASUAL
trainers MF
sweatshirt MF
sweatpants MF
T-shirt MF
polo-shirt MF
leather jacket MF
cardigan MF
cords M F
chinos M
jeans MF
denim skirt F

These are sample answers only; what people wear is changing constantly.

2 NA

3 NA

CHAPTER **SIX**   (37)

ACTIVITIES – STAGE **1**

1 NA

2 NA

3 SA:
Children were . . . sweet and innocent, and in no danger. Parents who allow them to play there are . . . irresponsible and thoughtless to expose them to possible harm.
Children are . . . being made lazy and stupid by watching television.
Parents are . . . also irresponsible and thoughtless for leaving them to watch television.

ACTIVITIES – STAGE **2**

1 Top picture: *worried, disapproving, concerned*
Bottom picture: *disgusted, horrified, sickened*

ACTIVITIES – STAGE **3**

1 NA

2 SA: fire, hot water, electricity, machinery, many others

3 Some dangers in the picture: hot water, electricity, deep water, knives, refrigerators, washing machines, ovens

ACTIVITIES – STAGE **4**

1 SA:
Children: 1–12
Boy: 1–12
Girl: 1–12
Old: 65+

2 English speakers do not agree about these words. They are grouped below as a general guide to meaning:

tot
toddler

youngster
juvenile
a youth
adolescent
kids
wet behind the ears

young adult
a man/woman in his/her prime

middle-aged
getting on a bit
a woman of a certain age
mid-life

senior citizen

elderly
past it

3 S (Slang): *tot, wet behind the ears, getting on a bit, past it.*
Others all E (Everyday English), though *kids* is borderline.

ACTIVITIES – STAGE 5

1 SA: Be careful, don't touch the
_____, stay away from the
_____, leave the
_____ alone, watch your
little brother/sister.

2 NA

3 Look out! Warning

Come in and Invitation
have a drink

Don't miss Advice
seeing the
Houses of
Parliament!

Add the Instruction
onions, and (recipe)
cook gently for
ten minutes.

Deliver us from Prayer
evil.

4 . . . many purposes, such as
warnings, invitations, advice, and
instructions, and even including
prayer . . .

CHAPTER **SEVEN** (44)

ACTIVITIES – STAGE 1

1 NA

2 SA: untidy, unconventional,
messy, odd

3 (a) ✗
(b) ✗
(c) ✗
(d) ✓
(e) ✓
(f) ✗

ACTIVITIES – STAGE 2

1 NA

2 These words describe the Tate
children: *choosy, self-centred, ill-
tempered, slovenly, fussy, withdrawn,
childish*

ACTIVITIES – STAGE 3

1 Holes; saying/answering/
speaking; unpleasant/
ill-tempered; sitting . . . straight

2 Bees *buzz*; the word also
describes telephone noises, many
people talking at once, and so
on.

3 NA

4 NA

CHAPTER **EIGHT** (52)

ACTIVITIES – STAGE 1

1 NA

2 Ivana Trump's language reveals
that she is not a native speaker,
and has not learned English well;
also that she clearly did not write
the book.

3 NA

ACTIVITIES – STAGE 2

1 Fragile grasp of English;
syntactically impaired; (obvious
English was not her first
language); limited linguistic
ability; avant-garde grammar

2 Ivana Trump's English is an
important part of the story
because she is presented as the
author of a book which she
could not possibly have written.

3 NA

4 NA

ACTIVITIES – STAGE 3

1 NA

2 Floozy: 0
Syntactically impaired woman: C
Lapsed billionaire: 0
Affluent trophy wife: C

ACTIVITIES – STAGE 4

1 The simple present; the present continuous

2 No: a mixture of simple present and simple past

3 SA: The writers use these tenses to give a sense of immediacy, to make the reader feel that the events are actually happening, and that the reader is present at the scene.

4 NA

5 NA

6 PRESENT SIMPLE

Functions:	Examples (SA):
An action planned for the future	He arrives on Thursday.
A habitual or permanent action or state	He lives in Brussels.
An action in the past, which the writer wants you to feel is happening now	Ivana Trump sits at a table, signing autographs.
An action happening at the moment of speaking	Becker serves. (TV or radio commentary)

PRESENT CONTINUOUS

An action planned for the future	He's flying to Brussels on Wednesday.
An action in the past, which the writer wants you to feel is happening now	Ivana Trump is wearing a grey dress.
An action happening at the moment of speaking	He's mowing the lawn; I can see him from here.
A temporary action or state, not necessarily happening at the moment of speaking	He's working for the World Bank.
A habitual action about which the speaker has powerful feelings	You're always using my car without asking me!

UNIT II

CHAPTER **ONE** (61)

ACTIVITIES – STAGE 1
1 NA
2 NA
3 (b), (c), (a)
4 (c)

ACTIVITIES – STAGE 2
1 He is typical.
2 Many examples. SA: *there have been rosier periods of history to live in than the last quarter of the 20th century . . . everywhere these days is somewhere else.*

ACTIVITIES – STAGE 3
1

augurs	Signs of the future
almshouses	Places specially built many years ago to house old people
hobble	Walk awkwardly because of an injury
vicar	A priest in the Church of England
observatory	A building in which scientists observe the stars
ingrained	Permanent, unlikely to change
earmarked	Put aside for a special purpose
premises	A house or other building

2 Likes: a local hospital which includes a casualty department; the almshouses; a school building which has a sign on it saying *school* and which actually is a school. Dislikes: a home computer centre; the planning department of the town hall; The Old Vicarage in which a retired civil servant lives; the used furniture depository.

3 SA:
(a) . . . this hospital had moved, too/had become an old people's home.
(b) . . . had been pulled down/destroyed/demolished.
(c) . . . it had become a home computer centre.
(d) . . . had moved to the new vicarage on the site of the old police station.
(e) . . . it had been replaced by the new vicarage.
(f) . . . had been pulled down/destroyed/demolished and the new police station built there.

4 NA
5 NA

ACTIVITIES – STAGE 4
1 NA
2 NA
3 NA

CHAPTER **TWO** (68)

ACTIVITIES – STAGE 1
1 NA
2 NA
3 NA
4 NA

ACTIVITIES – STAGE 2

1 NA

2 NA

3 SA: Stephanie Calman is an English woman of the younger generation, who because of her background is not typically British, and who challenges the idea that life was better before she was born, when people lived in happy communities.

4 NA

ACTIVITIES – STAGE 3

1 (c)

2 (c), (d), (e), (b), (a)

3 *One person*:   I, your identity
In between: non-parochial, European, community, the country, neighbours, continentals, local
Largest group: global, international, citizens of One World

ACTIVITIES – STAGE 4

1 NA

2 NA

CHAPTER **THREE**   (74)

ACTIVITIES – STAGE 1

1 NA

2 NA

3 NA

ACTIVITIES – STAGE 2

1 NA

2 NA

ACTIVITIES – STAGE 3

1 NA

2 *The town* surprisingly crowded; *the motel* expensive; *the bed* hard; *the TV reception* distorted; *the waitress* apparently unintelligent; *Bill Bryson's response* angry and revengeful

3 tarty; pummel; prised

4 tranquil; sinuous; tingle

5 NA

ACTIVITIES – STAGE 4

1 NA

2 NA

3 NA

CHAPTER **FOUR**   (80)

ACTIVITIES – STAGE 1

1 NA

2 TRAVELLERS (a), (d), (f), (g), (h) TOURISTS (b), (c), (e). (Students may disagree.)

ACTIVITIES – STAGE 2

1 NA

2 Matthew Parris and his friends seem to be travellers, because they do so many of the things listed for travellers in Activities, stage 1.

ACTIVITIES – STAGE 3

1 (b)

2 Good, unselfish behaviour; a good person; Ian; making the bus wait for a late passenger

3 NA

ACTIVITIES – STAGE 4

1 The passengers named the man El Gordo.

No one wanted El Gordo to sit by them.

El Gordo found a seat next to the Indian mother.

The Indian mother put her children into El Gordo's seat.

El Gordo ate a third helping of soup.

Ian shouted for the bus to stop.

El Gordo could not sit where he first sat.

El Gordo sat by Ian.

The bus climbed high into the mountains.

The weather became very cold.

Ian was the only warm person on the bus.

2 NA

3 NA

4 NA

ACTIVITIES – STAGE 5

1 NA

2 NA

CHAPTER **FIVE** (87)

ACTIVITIES – STAGE 1

1 NA

2 JOE AND JOANNE: *well-educated, tasteful, refined, well-dressed, sophisticated, travellers.*

OTHER AMERICANS ABROAD: *over-friendly, loud, brash, crude, vulgar, tourists.*

SA: When Joe and Joanne meet other Americans in England, they feel embarrassed, and hope that the Americans will not realize that Joe and Joanne are Americans, too. Joanne's husband, however, doesn't dislike Americans, and seems to think they are perfectly reasonable. Joe sometimes doesn't speak in front of Americans, hoping they won't know what he is. In the second scene, he goes further and actually pretends to be English.

ACTIVITIES – STAGE 2

1 *The place* Stratford-upon-Avon; *here* in England; *they'll* other Americans abroad; *Mary* Joe's wife (or partner); *the kids* the students Joe has brought to England; *James* Joanne's husband; *a machine* Joanne's telephone answering machine; *he* the actor shown in the programme; *they* the Royal Shakespeare Company in Stratford-upon-Avon.

2 SA:

JOE: Americans are not quite so ready to start talking to you in London as they are in Stratford.

JOE: I wish I lived in England like you, because living here is almost like being English.

JOANNE: It's a relief to have someone who understands how I feel about other Americans abroad.

JOE: Your husband probably makes more money than I do.

AMERICAN: I won't be able to show pictures of the actors in their costumes to the people back home.

AMERICAN: This game must be educational, since it comes from the Royal Shakespeare Company, but I don't understand what you learn from it.

3 (a) Joanne's programme for the students is what some other nations think is typical of highly-organized American travel.

(b) Similarly, the interest in what Joanne's husband earns is thought by some to be typically American.

ACTIVITIES – STAGE 3

1 NA

2 NA

3 NA

4 NA

ACTIVITIES – STAGE 4

1 NA

2 NA

CHAPTER SIX   (95)

ACTIVITIES – STAGE 1

1 NA

2 NA

3 NA

4 NA

5 The German-speaking Swiss; Turkish guest-workers in Germany; the Japanese; Vietnamese refugees in California; Tamils in Sri Lanka.

6 NA

ACTIVITIES – STAGE 2

1 (a) NA

(b) Religion and tradition and customs are the only two specifically mentioned.

(c) The answer suggests that Meera Syall and her family are now part of British

culture as well as Asian, and not so conscious of cultural differences.

2 Arranged marriage, assisted marriage; Meera Syall says assisted marriage is what is now done.

3 Because the geographical terms are now used to describe cultural differences.

ACTIVITIES – STAGE 3

1 NA

ACTIVITIES – STAGE 4

1 Probable: (g); improbable: (a), (b), (c), (d), (e), (f), (h)

2

Cousin Shaila	She wore . . .
A brute of a father	He is the person . . .
Sanjay	He is an imaginary . . .
Mrs A from Surrey	She is an imaginary . . .
Auntie Usha	She thinks Westerners . . .

ACTIVITIES – STAGE 5

1 (b), (c) – but students may disagree.

2 *Should, ought to*

3 NA

CHAPTER SEVEN   (103)

ACTIVITIES – STAGE 1

1 NA

2 NA

3 NA

4

PERSON	ATTITUDE
Vicki Woods	Generous, enthusiastic . . .

Her daughter	Fairly interested . . .
Her 14-year-old son	Uninterested . . .
Jeffrey Junior's mother	Highly nervous . . .

ACTIVITIES – STAGE 2

1 Likely: (a), (e), (f); unlikely: (b), (c), (d)

2 NA

3 NA

4 NA

ACTIVITIES – STAGE 3

1 NA

2 *tactfully* (a); *tuning up* (a); *raga* (b); *paediatrician* (b); *blushed* (a); *filthy* (b); *grimy* (b); *poked* (b); *stroked* (a); *tickled* (a); *shrieked* (a); *hampered* (a); *crone* (a).

3 NA

4 NA

ACTIVITIES – STAGE 4

1 NA

2 NA

3 NA

4 NA

CHAPTER **EIGHT**   (110)

ACTIVITIES – STAGE 1

1 NA

2 NA

ACTIVITIES – STAGE 2

1 (b)

2
England is now . . .	3
The idea we met . . .	1
British lower class . . .	0
British working class . . .	0

Peregrine Worsthorne . . .	0
Margaret Thatcher . . .	2
The bravery . . .	3
British class tastes . . .	1

3 NA

ACTIVITIES – STAGE 3

1 (a) The opinions . . . an official paper from the British government.

(b) The Italians . . . angry.

(c) The attitude . . . based on stereotypes and unflattering.

(d) The document . . . had a political system the Italians admired.

ACTIVITIES – STAGE 4

1 NA

2 NA

3

NOUN	ADJECTIVE	MEANING
frivolity	frivolous	not serious
taciturnity	taciturn	silent
spontaneity	spontaneous	acting from natural feelings, without planning
dishonesty	dishonest	not honest, likely to lie or cheat
hypocrisy	hypocritical	saying one thing but doing another
mendacity	mendacious	not truthful, lying
insincerity	insincere	not sincere, not real, true or honest
bravery	brave	without fear
unreliability	unreliable	not reliable, not to be trusted
punctuality	punctual	not late, always on time
vivacity	vivacious	full of life and energy

eccentricity	eccentric	peculiar, unusual
ingenuity	ingenious	clever at making or inventing things
creativity	creative	with the ability to create new things and ideas
stupidity	stupid	silly, foolish, not intelligent
indomitability	indomitable	too strong to be stopped or defeated
impassivity	impassive	not showing (or not having) feelings

4 NA
5 NA

CHAPTER **NINE**   (119)

ACTIVITIES – STAGE 1

1 immigrant; alien; expatriate; outsider; authorities; officialese; jargon; fill; forms; documents; testimonials; affidavits; permit; naturalized; citizen; native; assimilated; passport; bureaucracy; officialdom

☐   ☐

2 Examples: increase, increase;

☐   ☐ ☐   ☐

object, object; rebel, rebel

ACTIVITIES – STAGE 2

1 NA
2 NA
3 NA
4 NA

5 NA
6 NA
7 Some things the texts have in common: both are about people who are not American trying to deal with the INS (the Immigration and Naturalization Service), part of the American government.

Some differences: Jonathan Wilson is in Boston, was English, and actually becomes an American citizen after taking a test. He overheard some interviews and realized that the test was more difficult than he had thought. He just managed to pass. He then met his congressional representative, and, as a US citizen, complained to him about the test.

Kennedy Fraser is in New York (and from the reference to the handbag (line 24) is presumably a woman); she is a Permanent Resident Alien, whose green card – her permit – is so old she has to get it renewed. The article does not say she seeks citizenship. It is about the terrible conditions in which applicants like herself have to wait, how badly they are treated, and about all the services offered – many of them doubtful – to make the process easier.

ACTIVITIES – STAGE 3

1 NA
2 NA

ACTIVITIES – STAGE 4

1 NA
2 NA

UNIT III

CHAPTER **ONE** (129)

ACTIVITIES – STAGE 1

1 SA:

The women's movement	Women are valuing themselves and their work more highly than before.
Genetic engineering	Scientists are making discoveries which may make it possible to decide in advance what your child will be like.
Environmental concern	Pollution and thoughtless consumption are threatening many wild species, and perhaps the human race.

2 Countable: advance, species, rights, threat, identity, increase, status, gene, planet, environment, discovery.
Uncountable: pollution, equality, discrimination, engineering, wildlife, destruction, research.

3 Countable singular: *a/an, every*
Countable plural: *few, a few, several, many, enough, most, all, a lot of*
Uncountable: *much, little/a little, enough, most, all, a lot of*
All: *the, any, some*

4 With definite article: the changing status of women; the future of genetic engineering; the way men see themselves; the pollution of the environment; the threat to tradition from gene research; the preservation of wildlife; the discovery of how our genes work; the recent advance in sexual equality; the future of our planet.

5 Something in the construction – an adjective, or a phrase introduced by prepositions *of, to, in* – limits the meaning from the general to the particular.
Teachers may want to explore this more using grammar books.

ACTIVITIES – STAGE 2

1 NA
2 NA
3 NA
4 NA

ACTIVITIES – STAGE 3

1 All except dare/dare not are possible. Even that is *just* possible.

2 Underline: may/may not; could/couldn't; might/might not. All others (see 1) are possible, but these will work best in the next exercise.

3 NA

ACTIVITIES – STAGE 4

1 NA
2 NA

CHAPTER **TWO**   (135)

ACTIVITIES – STAGE **1**

1 NA

2 NA

3 NA

ACTIVITIES – STAGE **2**

1 NA

2 Philip Norman . . . was first unenthusiastic . . .
The salesman . . . had a fake expression . . .
Mrs Philip Norman . . . was horrified . . .
The elderly lady . . . loved the portable telephone . . .
The female publicity director in N.Y. . . . was suspicious . . .
The cat . . . was sick
The New York publishing director . . . had wonderful news . . .

ACTIVITIES – STAGE **3**

1 NA

2 NA

3 (a), (f)

4 Ways of walking: *striding, plodded*; sounds: *purr* (cat) *crackled* (electronic) *gasp* (person); company symbol: *sprite mascot*; old shoes: *scuffed*; gesture: *shoo*; very upset: *devastated*.

5 NA

6 NA

CHAPTER **THREE**   (142)

ACTIVITIES – STAGE **1**

1 NA

2 NA

ACTIVITIES – STAGE **2**

1 NA

2 032838: Wendy Cope, the writer of the poem
027564: another writer she meets at the publishers' party
036040: another writer she meets at the publishers' party
    014: another writer – someone says he is second-rate

ACTIVITIES – STAGE **3**

1 *They*: Wendy Cope's publishers
The probable speaker: 036040
The speaker . . . : Wendy Cope's publishers

2 (a) II
   (b) III
   (c) I

ACTIVITIES – STAGE **4**

1 032838 and 036040 have the same rhythm

2 NA

3 NA

4 NA

ACTIVITIES – STAGE **5**

1 327,564 is shown by the comma to be a measurement.

2 NA

3 Zero, nought, nil; we probably use these either when the 0 stands alone, or to make it clear to our listeners when there is some doubt. We don't say the 0 separately when it comes in the middle of an amount or measurement – but it changes the amount, of course, from tens to hundreds, and so on.

4 NA

5 NA

6 Point; twenty-seven point five
three.

7 Plus; minus; times; equals; at; per
cent.

8 Five hundred and twenty-six
pounds and ninety-eight pence.
A (or one) hundred and forty-
three thousand, five hundred and
sixty dollars and fifty cents.

ACTIVITIES – STAGE 6

1 NA

2 NA

CHAPTER **FOUR**   (148)

ACTIVITIES – STAGE 1

1 NA

2 NA

ACTIVITIES – STAGE 2

1 NA

2 SA:
Calvin Trillin, an older
American man, found the word
gormless in an English newspaper
while visiting some friends in
London. His daughters would
probably have defined it as *ditz-
brained*. From the text we also
learn that English people prefer
toast old and dry; that American
policemen are called *cops*; that
Margaret Thatcher was her
country's *supremo*; and that
gormless is an old word, first used
in 1746.

ACTIVITIES – STAGE 3

1 NA

2 *gormless* (f)
ditz-brained (e)
supremo (d)

lineup (g)
raver (b)
sitcom (a)
cagmag (c)

3 racks (line 11); pitchfork(s) (line
29); marginally (line 21); facile
(line 26); dowdy (line 30); quaint
(line 29); antique (line 29);
subculture (line 40)

ACTIVITIES – STAGE 4

1 colloquial (f); idiomatic (h);
idiom (g); technical (b); jargon (c);
dialect (e); humorous (d);
pompous (a); archaic (j);
obsolete (i).

2 SA: *ditz-brained* is probably usable
only by young people to friends
of their own age in everyday
conversations or informal letters.

3 Two fifteen-year-old boys:
nitwit . . .
A government document:
mentally disadvantaged
One woman . . . : *that stupid ass*
A teacher. . . : *a bit slow*
An English employer . . . :
gormless
An article . . . : *of less than average* . . .
These are sample answers; you may
disagree.

ACTIVITIES – STAGE 5

1 NA

2 NA

3 NA

ACTIVITIES – STAGE 6

1 *acid house party* (b), (c); *boxers* (g);
care card (a), (b); *clergyperson* (e),
(h); *faxphone* (a); *to greenlight* (d);
lager lout (b), (c); *ozone-friendly*
(f), (c); *sound-bite* (b), (c);
thirtysomething (b), (h).

2 NA

CHAPTER **FIVE**   (158)

ACTIVITIES – STAGE **1**
1 NA

2 NA

ACTIVITIES – STAGE **2**
1 NA

2 1992; *Time Takes Time*;
Gothenburg (Sweden); x; 1965;
x; drum(s); drum(s); three; only
John Lennon's full name appears
in the article – and the surname
of Paul McCartney – George
Harrison's name does not appear.

ACTIVITIES – STAGE **3**
1 NA

2 SA: *sharp, light, witty, deft,
forthright, idiomatic, direct*

3 Past (a), (d), (f), (h); Present (b),
(i), (j); Future (c), (e), (g)

4 NA

ACTIVITIES – STAGE **4**
1 NA

2 *Catch the Word*: translates pop
songs . . .
Pop Words: explains the English
words . . .
Oh Carolina: a Number One hit
by Shaggy
Shaggy: Jamaican-born ragga
singer
Carolina: Shaggy's girlfriend
squirrel: small furry animal . . .
Damn! I Wish I Was Your Lover:
song by Sophie B. Hawkins

3 *intricacies* complicated meanings
pukka   good, of high quality
vagaries unusual or unexpected
          ideas and acts
prosaic down-to-earth, everyday

*come under
the microscope* be looked at closely
*definitive
interpretations* serious and final
                statements . . .
jungle images word-pictures of
                things . . .
modicum   a certain small
                amount . . .

4 Five and a half million; fifteen
minutes; he means he likes the
way Carolina dances;
Damn! I Wish I was Your Lover;
sex, drugs, the truly weird.

ACTIVITIES – STAGE **5**
1 NA

2 The line should be high around
1965, and begin to drop around
1985. Otherwise, it is open to
class discussion.

ACTIVITIES – STAGE **6**
1 NA

2 (a) Rod Stewart, line 6; (b) the
Beatles, the Rolling Stones,
Elton John, Culture Club,
Duran Duran, line 15; (c)
Clapton, John, Collins,
Stewart, line 20; (d)
Germany, line 33; (e) The
Netherlands, Sweden and
Iceland, line 36; (f) Mexico,
South Korea and Taiwan,
line 40; (g) Japan, line 41.

3 NA

4 SA: partly; even; not;
currently/now;
proportion/part/share;
dropping/falling; long; reason;
dominate; field; world/globe;
formerly; obliged/bound;
export/sell.

ACTIVITIES – STAGE 7
1 NA
2 NA
3 NA

CHAPTER **SIX** (171)

ACTIVITIES – STAGE 1
1 NA
2 NA
3 (a) NA
  (b) SA: . . . are aggressive, and that the hostility they express is directed at him.

ACTIVITIES – STAGE 2
1 Numbering from left to right, top row to bottom row:
1 (c) 2 (i) 3 (g) 4 (h) 5 (d) 6 (?)
7 (e) 8 (?) 9 (a) 10 (k) 11 (f) 12 (j)
13 (b) 14 (b).

2 NA
3 (a) 'Don't mess with [muss] me' – line 15.
  (b) signalling a state of stoned acquiescence – line 20.
  (c) Native American haircuts (hostile to white invaders and swindlers) – line 45.
  (d) Rocker haircuts (hostile to family values, bourgeois repression, and regular hours) – line 47.
  (e) English punk haircuts (hostile to the upper class and fans at foreign soccer teams) – line 48.
  (f) American punk haircuts (hostile to Mom, Dad, and high-school dress codes) – line 50.

4 NA

5 A *simmer* is a heat just below boiling, suggesting the men are easily moved to violence. *Muss* deepens the meaning of *mess* as well as echoing some of its sounds, and so adds to the richness of the passage.

Leonine means lion-like; the word *mane* describes the hair around a lion's head. *Samsonesque* comes from the story of Samson, the secret of whose strength was in his hair.

Venetian blinds allow people to control the exact amount of light coming through windows, as the librarian tries to do with her hostility. She is sweet-mannered (line 35) and twinkles behind her glasses (line 38), so she is not totally hostile.

6 NA
7 NA

ACTIVITIES – STAGE 3
1 NA
2 NA
3 NA
4 NA
5 NA

CHAPTER **SEVEN** (178)

ACTIVITIES – STAGE 1
1 *Lifestyle* appears in the 1990 edition of the *Longman Register of New Words* as (noun): 'A marketing concept in which a range of products is designed and packaged . . . in such a way as to fit in with the potential customers' self-image and the

sort of life they think of
themselves as leading'.

Most people assume *lifestyle* to
include not only hair, clothes,
house, furnishings and car, but
how people live – hours of
work, leisure activities, partners,
children.

2 NA

3 NA

ACTIVITIES – STAGE 2

1 *New man* (*Register of New Words*,
1990): 'A man who does not
adopt an aggressively male social
role, but participates in activities
traditionally regarded as more
appropriate to women (e.g.
looking after children, cooking
and housework.)'

2 (c)

3 (b); (d); (c); (e); (a).

ACTIVITIES – STAGE 3

1 (b); (a); (a); (b).

2 (a) I; (b) III; (c) VII; (d) V; (e) VI;
(f) VIII; (g) II; (h) IV.

3 NA

4 Other jobs mentioned: laundry
(washing clothes), cooking,
cleaning, clearing out the car,
grocery shopping planning

5 NA

6 NA

ACTIVITIES – STAGE 4

1 NA

2 NA

3 The present continuous form
usually indicates the more
serious, fixed arrangements.

4 NA

5 NA

6 NA

ACKNOWLEDGEMENTS

The publishers make grateful ackowledgement to the following for permission to reproduce copyright material:

Christopher Isherwood, *Goodbye to Berlin*, Chatto & Windus, London; Ogden Nash, 'The Germ' from *Bed Riddance*, André Deutsch Ltd, London; Miles Kington, 'At the mercy of a child's plastic sword', *The Independent*, 31 March 1992; Henry Beard and Christopher Cerf, *The Official Politically Correct Dictionary and Handbook*, HarperCollins Publishers Ltd, London; Charles Laurence, 'Mural for restaurant gets artist in dogfight', *Daily Telegraph*, 18 October 1993, © The Telegraph plc, London, 1993; George Bernard Shaw, 'Sir, The Opera management at Covent Garden regulates the dress of its male patrons . . . ' from *Shaw's Music*, The Society of Authors on behalf of the Bernard Shaw Estate; Posy Simmonds, 'Lost Eden', *Guardian*, 21 November 1992, by permission of the artist; Alison Lurie, *Love and Friendship*, William Heinemann Ltd, London; Alison Lurie, *The War Between the Tates*, William Heinemann Ltd, London; Richard Guilliat, 'It's a vunderful, vunderful book', *The Independent*, 13 April 1992; Pont, 'The British Character' from The British Character and the World of Pont, Element Books Ltd, Dorset; Stephanie Calman, 'Local body in identity crisis', *The Times*, 16 June 1990, by permission of the author; Bill Bryson, *The Lost Continent*, Martin Secker & Warburg Ltd, London; Matthew Parris, *Inca-Kola*, Weidenfeld & Nicolson, London; Richard Nelson, *Some Americans Abroad*, Faber & Faber Ltd, London; Meera Syall, 'Arranged Marriage', by permission of the author; Vicki Wood, 'Hands off my baby', *The Spectator*; Sonia Purnell, 'They are loud, late and don't tell the truth', *Daily Telegraph*, 8 December 1993, © The Telegraph plc, London, 1993; Jonathan Wilson, 'Expatriate Games', *The New Yorker*, 5 July 1993, © 1993 Jonathan Wilson; Kennedy Fraser, 'Waiting in room 3-120', *The New Yorker*, 11 January 1993, © 1993 Kennedy Fraser; Ros Chast, 'The world's first genetically engineered human hits adolescence', © 1993 The New Yorker Magazine Inc; Donald Reilly, 'Books by men are in the basement', © 1993 The New Yorker Magazine Inc; Dedini, 'But can they save themselves?', © 1983 The New Yorker Magazine Inc; W. Miller, 'I was sad because I had no . . . no mobile phone', © 1993 The New Yorker Magazine Inc; Philip Norman, 'On life without a flex', *Independent Magazine*, 23 January 1993; Wendy Cope, 'Reflections on a Royalty Statement' from *Making Cocoa for Kingsley Amis*, Faber & Faber Ltd, London; Calvin Trillin, 'Broken English', *The New Yorker*, 23 November 1992, © 1992 Calvin Trillin; Giles Smith, 'Ringo Starr talks to Giles Smith about shaking off the past', *The Independent*, 16 April 1992; Louise Gray, 'If all you hear is radio gaga . . ., Pop On Friday', *The Times*, 28 January 1994,

© Times Newspapers Ltd, 1994; Jim White, 'In 1965 fifteen of the thirty best-selling US singles were British . . .', *The Independent*, 23 February 1994; John Updike, 'Hostile Haircuts', *The New Yorker*, 2 November 1992, © 1992 John Updike; Maurice Vellecoop, 'Hostile Haircuts' cartoon, *The New Yorker*, 2 November 1992; Ruth Picardie, 'Not quite New Man but less of a chore than sloth', *The Independent*, 25 February 1994.

Acknowledgements for cartoons by Mel Calman: p. 170, from *Calman at the Royal Opera House*, J. M. Dent & Sons, London.

Every effort has been made to trace the copyright holder in every case. The publishers would be interested to hear from any not acknowledged here.